Bible Interpretations

Sixth Series

September 25 - December 18, 1892

I Corinthians, Acts, Luke

Bible Interpretations

Sixth Series

I Corinthians, Acts, Luke

These Bible Interpretations were given during the early eighteen nineties at the Christian Science Theological Seminary at Chicago, Illinois. This Seminary was independent of the First Church of Christ Scientist in Boston, Mass.

By

Emma Curtis Hopkins

President of the Christian Science Theological Seminary at Chicago, Illinois

Wise Woman Press

Bible Interpretations: Sixth Series

By Emma Curtis Hopkins

© WiseWoman Press

Managing Editor: Michael Terranova

ISBN: 978-0945385-56-1

WiseWoman Press

Portland, OR 97217

www.wisewomanpress.com

www.emmacurtishopkins.com

CONTENTS

	Foreword by Rev. Natalie R. Jean v
	Introduction by Rev. Michael Terranova 1
I.	THE SCIENCE OF CHRIST .... 6 *I Corinthians 11:23-34*
II.	ON THE HEALING OF SAUL .... 19 *Acts 9:1-31*
III.	The Power of Mind Explained .... 31 *Acts 9:32-43*
IV.	FAITH IN GOOD TO COME .... 41 *Acts 10:1-20*
V.	EMERSON'S GREAT TASK .... 48 *Acts 10:30-48*
VI.	THE TEACHING OF FREEDOM .... 56 *Acts 11:19-30*
VII.	SEEK AND YE SHALL FIND .... 64 *Acts 12:1-17*
VIII.	THE MINISTRY OF THE HOLY MOTHER .... 71 *Acts 13:1-13*
IX.	POWER OF LOFTY IDEAS .... 83 *Acts 13:26-43*
X.	SURE RECIPE FOR OLD AGE .... 91 *Acts 13:44-52 Acts 14:1-7*
XI.	THE HEALING PRINCIPLE .... 98 *Acts 14:8-22*
XII.	WASHINGTON'S VISION .... 107 *Acts 15:12-29*
XIII.	Review of The Twelve Lessons 117
XIV.	SHEPHERDS AND THE STAR .... 127 *Luke 2:8-20*
	List of Bible Interpretation Series 134

Foreword

By Rev. Natalie R. Jean

I have read many teachings by Emma Curtis Hopkins, but the teachings that touch the very essence of my soul are her Bible Interpretations. There are many books written on the teachings of the Bible, but none can touch the surface of the true messages more than these Bible interpretations. With each word you can feel and see how Spirit spoke through Emma. The mystical interpretations take you on a wonderful journey to Self Realization.

Each passage opens your consciousness to a new awareness of the realities of life. The illusions of life seem to disappear through each interpretation. Emma teaches that we are the key that unlocks the doorway to the light that shines within. She incorporates ideals of other religions into her teachings, in order to understand the commonalities, so that there is a complete understanding of our Oneness. Emma opens our eyes and mind to a better today and exciting future.

Emma Curtis Hopkins, one of the Founders of New Thought teaches us to love ourselves, to speak our Truth, and to focus on our Good. My life has moved in wonderful directions because of her teachings. I know the only thing that can move me in this world is God. May these interpretations guide you to a similar path and may you truly remember that "There Is Good For You and You Ought to Have It."

Introduction

Emma Curtis Hopkins was born in 1849 in Killingsly, Connecticut. She passed on April 8, 1925. Mrs. Hopkins had a marvelous education and could read many of the worlds classical texts in their original language. During her extensive studies she was always able to discover the Universal Truths in each of the world's sacred traditions. She quotes from many of these teachings in her writings. As she was a very private person, we know little about her personal life. What we do know has been gleaned from other people or from the archived writings we have been able to discover.

Emma Curtis Hopkins was one of the greatest influences on the New Thought movement in the United States. She taught over 50,000 people the Universal Truth of knowing "God is All there is." She taught many of founders of early New Thought, and in turn these individuals expanded the influence of her teachings. All of her writings encourage the student to enter into a personal relationship with God. She presses us to deny anything except the Truth of this spiritual Presence in every area of our lives. This is the central focus of all her teachings.

The first six series of Bible Interpretations were presented at her seminary in Chicago, Illinois. The remaining Series', probably close to thirty, were printed in the Inter Ocean Newspaper in Chicago. Many of the lessons are no longer available for various reasons. It is the intention of WiseWoman Press to publish as many of these Bible Interpretations as possible. Our hope is that any missing lessons will be found or directed to us.

I am very honored to join the long line of people that have been involved in publishing Emma Curtis Hopkins's Bible Interpretations. Some confusion exists as to the numbering sequence of the lessons. In the early 1920's many of the lessons were published by the Highwatch Fellowship. Inadvertently the first two lessons were omitted from the numbering system. Rev. Joanna Rogers has corrected this mistake by finding the first two lessons and restoring them to their rightful place in the order. Rev. Rogers has been able to find many of the missing lessons at the International New Thought Alliance archives in Mesa, Arizona. Rev. Rogers painstakingly scoured the archives for the missing lessons as well as for Mrs. Hopkins other works. She has published much of what was discovered. WiseWoman Press is now publishing the correctly numbered series of the Bible Interpretations.

In the early 1940's, there was a resurgence of interest in Emma's works. At that time, Highwatch Fellowship began to publish many of her writings, and it was then that *High Mysticism*, her seminal work was published. Previously, the material contained in High Mysticism was only available as individual lessons and was brought together in book form for the first time. Although there were many errors in these first publications and many Bible verses were incorrectly quoted, I am happy to announce that WiseWoman Press is now publishing *High Mysticism* in the a corrected format. This corrected form was scanned faithfully from the original, individual lessons.

The next person to publish some of the Bible Lessons was Rev. Marge Flotron from the Ministry of Truth International in Chicago, Illinois. She published the Bible Lessons as well as many of Emma's other works. By her initiative, Emma's writings were brought to a larger audience when DeVorss & Company, a longtime publisher of Truth Teachings, took on the publication of her key works.

In addition, Dr. Carmelita Trowbridge, founding minister of The Sanctuary of Truth in Alhambra, California, inspired her assistant minister, Rev. Shirley Lawrence, to publish many of Emma's works, including the first three series of Bible Interpretations. Rev. Lawrence created mail order courses for many of these Series. She has graciously passed on any information she had, in order to assure that these works continue to inspire individuals and groups who are called to further study of the teachings of Mrs. Hopkins.

Finally, a very special acknowledgement goes to Rev Natalie Jean, who has worked diligently to retrieve several of Emma's lessons from the Library of Congress, as well as libraries in Chicago. Rev. Jean hand-typed many of the lessons she found on microfilm. Much of what she found is on her website, www.highwatch.net.

It is with a grateful heart that I am able to pass on these wonderful teachings. I have been studying dear Emma's works for fifteen years. I was introduced to her writings by my mentor and teacher, Rev. Marcia Sutton. I have been overjoyed with the results of delving deeply into these Truth Teachings.

In 2004, I wrote a Sacred Covenant entitled "Resurrecting Emma," and created a website, www.emmacurtishopkins.com. The result of creating this covenant and website has brought many of Emma's works into my hands and has deepened my faith in God. As a result of my love for these works, I was led to become a member of WiseWoman Press and to publish these wonderful teachings. God is Good.

My understanding of Truth from these divinely inspired teachings keeps bringing great Joy, Freedom, and Peace to my life.

Dear reader; It is with an open heart that I offer these works to you, and I know they will touch you as they have touched me. Together we are living in the Truth that God is truly present, and living for and through each of us.

The greatest Truth Emma presented to us is "My Good is my God, Omnipresent, Omnipotent and Omniscient."

Rev. Michael Terranova
WiseWoman Press
Vancouver, Washington, 2010

LESSON I

THE SCIENCE OF CHRIST

I Corinthians 11:23-34

    D'Albert treated with coldness a brilliant young man who had solved a difficult problem in mathematics, because he told him he had worked it out to earn a seat in the French Academy. "You will never get on with that motive in your mind," said D'Albert. Looking over the busy students in a normal school I metaphysically perceived a certain number of them working up their notes with the sole idea of making their living by and by as capable expounders of the propositions under consideration. I did not feel on the purposely sensitized plate of my mind any reflection of actual interest in the subject they were treating.

    A sharp and fearless critic of human motives said to a band of reformers that "if all the saloons, etc., were closed up in a night the reformers would be the maddest lot of people in the world," because

"Othello's occupation would be gone". Some people have gone so far as to believe that the doctors would be a very disappointed set if all the people in the world were to be made perfectly well in an instant

The Science of Christ teaches that we live on our motives. If our motives are to get bread and clothes and good repute in the world, we may get these things, but there will still be left a hunger, a nakedness, a loneliness which externals cannot satisfy. D'Albert meant to inform the young man that the real honors of the Academy were won only by those who loved mathematical principles for their own sake. There is an initiation by motive, which is the esoteric doctrine open to all peoples of all tongues who love the doctrine for its own sake. It takes only a few words for the "Initiated" to perceive their own kind in a speaker. A brilliant list of accomplishments is not the entrance ticket to the ranks of the truly esoteric.

When accomplishments by which you make your external living have failed you, if then you have felt the love of the Jesus Christ principles for their own sake that love will attend to your living. If you can at once drop the idea of depending at all upon any external performance, but kindly engage in each duty as not essential to your support, or defense, or life, or health, or peace, your "seat in the Academy" will be given you at once. Your house external will be shown you. The idea of "making your living" will not be in your mind.

Riding on the train you pay for your fare because the conductor has faced you with "Ticket, please!" while you were trying to avoid having to pay your fare. The payment of the fifty cents has nothing to do with the case a year from that time when you lose a hundred dollars; for you are living by your motives, not by the outer transactions. Some are faced up soon with their motives, some late, but there is a harvest from motives ahead of us all.

Science is science, and whether it is the Jesus Christ Principle of Life we are working out, or the mathematical principles of abstruse equations, we are "initiated" by love of principle and not by a trick of computations. The golden text of today's lesson contains this same idea. It makes mention of the outer performance of right actions with which the outer church is satisfied, and the inner performance with ideas with which Principle, the true church, is satisfied. The text reads, *"Let a man examine himself, and so let him eat of that Bread and drink of that Cup"*. The lesson is found in (I Cor. 11:23-34). It tells of breaking the body of Jesus Christ. There is a very visible meaning to breaking the body, and a very deep or esoteric meaning. The visible meaning is that the body of Christ is His doctrine. Whoever believes His doctrine in his heart eats His body.

The esoteric sense describes the effect of believing His doctrine. It coincides with the "Bhagavad-Gita" teachings of "attachments". The mind gets "attached" to ideas. The mind gets glued to notions. According to these attachments our "body" or quality of character is made up. The Jesus Christ doctrine eaten till it is bone of our bone and flesh of our flesh causes us to be "broken up" over and over.

The Jesus Christ doctrine does not let us get crystallized to anything. We cannot remember the past with either joy or sorrow. "Leave the things that are behind." It will not let us form the habit of anticipating the future. If we get to looking forward we get "attached" to the future. This looking forward is sure to result in a timid apprehensiveness or dread as we put forward our thoughts into it. The Jesus Christ doctrine, or body, breaks us up often when we eat it. It is itself broken into omnipresent ideas for omni-eating. It touches the tiniest event of each day to quicken it with life. It vivifies the dreams of our nights with omniscience. It takes away our memories of past events and people. It astonishes us with knowledge of present meanings of actions small and great. It gives us sight of the harvest of motives. It satisfies us with the outcome of ideas.

Through not eating the doctrine of Jesus Christ, but trying to impress the history of a personality upon itself, Paul says that the church is "weak, sickly, and asleep". He lays stress upon the principle of not judging of our neighbor's actions because our own actions cannot be judged by them. The people who spend much time memorizing external facts about things suddenly find their minds broken up and they remember nothing. If they have not identified themselves with the principles for which those external facts stand, they get the reputation of being old, or brain-cracked, or crazy. It was an unworthy eating and drinking of life events that they indulged in. They missed the meanings, and must be counted in with the gluttons and wine bibbers of scripture as much as if they had spent their minds thinking of old and new wines, different kinds of roasts, and delicate fries.

There is but one subject with which the mind can be legitimately employed. That is pure Principle. "What principle is involved?" we must ask. The principle being true we proceed to think it. We become it by thinking it. Now, Principle never gets old or cracks. So we, being Principle by thinking it, never get old or cracked.

If any sage or saint has the reputation of being aged, or having lost his mind, we may know at once that he occupied his mind with ideas of externals. He must have said a great deal about what it was religious to eat and not to eat. He must have tried to explain whether people should wear long or short hair, red or black dresses. He very likely trimmed his sails to keep in with people who knew about art, literature, finance, not drinking the knowledge that the principle we are occupying our mind which takes care of our comrades for us, and finds our proper seats in the right places.

One who lately drank the blood of pure doctrine (using Paul's figure) found his family afraid to buy certain articles for fear they might fail to pay a coming note. He told them to buy what was needed for the house and let the future obligation take care of itself. He felt that by laying up for the future they fastened themselves into it to the discomfort of the present, which would certainly have the effect upon his family that it has had upon the church, so glued to its hopes of a future — appearing Jesus Christ — viz., "Weakness, sickness, sleep" (or loss of miracle-working energy). He saw that the doctrine of Jesus broke up his old "attachment" to laying up for a future.

The true doctrine breaks up all our old notions, but leaves us stronger and stauncher for the breaking. Facts about Pericles, Plutarch, Phidas, Philo, statistics of drunkards, records of cholera ravages, are very husky eating. They have no blood in them. They too, break us up, but they leave us blanks; we have to put out groping fingers after something we know not what. "Infants crying for the light, and with no language but a cry."

Pure doctrine eaten and drunk by us breaks up our notions and rolls them as debris down the stream of our principles. We find that if we suddenly see into a principle, everything that occurs immediately after that insight is the effect of that insight. For instance, you suddenly perceive that the reason why we have strikes is because the church has taught that man is under the curse but sometime he will be free, instead of proclaiming that this day is every man free; you see the contracting effect of belief in the fall of man, so that some of us have fallen below each other in the scales and are subject one to another. You see how ideas go over the world, crossing and recrossing each other in the minds of people who cannot imagine how they came by them, till the Jesus Christ doctrine of all being born of God from the beginning cuts some of the cords of the prevailing ideas and makes men feel that they have as good a right to peace and freedom as their neighbors. You see how working along on the externals by establishing charity houses and handcuffing criminals will never work the amelioration and reforms hoped for, you realize how definitely some strong mind must now set going the clear cut statements of the Absolute Truth.

Well, the clear realization of all this, by one bold mental stroke, will knock off a dozen of your friends, tear up some of your estates by the roots, grind some of your fairest hopes to powder. But this pure knowledge of pure Principle, which will roll so much debris about your head, will also roll to you along its vitalizing stream some comrades whom winds cannot shake, some fortunes which come straight from lovers of your ideas, some new prospects for your family with unassailable strength in their excellence.

He that would save himself from the action of Principle had better not enter upon the study thereof; he had better play around among externals holding his goods by the skittish tenure of materiality. This is what Paul means by saying that we should not be judged with the world. The same sloughing off of existing conditions takes place with people who deal with externals, because it is the nature of externals to change. The difference between the ups and downs of things under the law of materiality trusted, and pure Principle understood, is that the substance of things is more clearly felt and seen by those who get everything broken up by the stream of their true ideas, while they who trust in material ways see nothing except their losses.

We cannot judge by appearances, and the mere effort to do so is "eating and drinking to damnation, not discerning the Lord's body".

A minister of the strict sort declared that he was so opposed to spiritual healing that he would rather his own beloved parents should "die" than be treated by such a practice. Not long after one of his parents suddenly "sickened and died". Had he known how arable, how fertile the soil of an intense or excited state of mind is to carry out suggestions he would not have said that.

The one who believes in Christ as a principle of healing ever present among us is eating of the Lord's body. He who does not so believe is "eating damnation", so Paul says. He means that his words come to pass upon himself and his affairs exactly the same as do the words of those who speak Truth, but that one goes out in nothingness, while the other lives. He tells us that if we hunger we had better eat at home. The deeper meaning of this idea is that before we get out among people we had better rouse our minds to the most perfect conclusions we can decide upon, which we would wish to see come to pass, and then speak some strong words to bring them to pass in our lot.

If we wait to speak Absolute Principles when occasions arise among our neighbors we may eat too greedily to "condemnation"; that is, we may speak what we will wish we had not when our neighbors arouse our feelings. It is not a good manner of "eating" to speak forth that it "seemed as if we should die", when we relate some anecdote or describe our sensations, for that speech will bring up an occasion when it will verily seem as if we would die. If the minister had thought it all over carefully before he committed himself to eating such words we would not have spoken them into the soil of a hothouse to bring down his father so soon.

According to Jesus Christ there is no reality whatsoever in the fruits of false or foolish words, but they seem very real indeed, and as there is a scientific way of averting the shades of error we are here advised to take it. A lad took the positive word one day in the company of some grown friends that he would always be lucky. Immediately afterwards a piece of good fortune came to him, seemingly by reason of his wise exertions. A metaphysician told him it was because he spoke so sturdily while he was in company with others. He could not see how it was because of what he had spoken a month before when it was, as it seemed to him, wholly due to his "hustling at the right moment". "Your hustling would have come to nothing if you had called yourself unlucky when you were in the presence of other minds," insisted the metaphysician; "your words are always going before you and lighting on your opportunities."

This is exactly what the thirty-fourth verse of this lesson means, whether Paul got so deeply into its meaning or not. Jesus told them to enter the closet and get it settled in their minds what they wanted to have brought to pass before they got out among men; then, when excited, they would fill the rich moment with rich seeds. Higher than the flights of the archangels sings the meaning of every Scripture text; down among the brooms and spades of the peasant's cottage rustle the wings of the angels of comfort these texts send forth. There is no moment when the white mercy of God is not touching each feeling, each word, with opportunity to make life a manifest garden of peace.

This lesson is called a temperance lesson. It is a perfect temperance lesson, because it insists upon our eating and drinking right ideas at home so that when we get among people we shall eat and drink with great results. You will notice that

Paul does not tell them not to meet together to eat because he knows that words spoken in moments of excitement in the presence of others count so powerfully. He simply tells us to get our minds settled on the ideas which we would like to see carried out, and then we shall not be off guard when we get talking in company.

Another thing about eating at home first is that the ideas which we have thought profoundly have a more enduring demonstration when they come to pass. If the boy had thought out that idea that he must always be fortunate on the principle that he knew God as the provider, and that God could not fail, his speech to his friends would fasten to an enduring demonstration of success, having an everlasting reason for the hope that was in him — not transient prosperity, like a hothouse rose that blooms to fade quickly.

In explaining Bible texts do not stop at their outer meaning. Push them to metaphysical or esoteric meanings. Compel them to explain your commonest emotions. Find how they teach your mind to conceive its own law of easy mastery over your lot. You do not need to be always grubbing and toiling and moiling while your neighbors lie in hammocks at the seaside, if you will understand the Bible. You do not need to have that dark cloud hanging over your life which makes your riches such a mockery. You do not need to dread forever something, you cannot tell what. You do not need to be glued to any of these things. They will loose from your life with your understanding of the esoterics of the Scripture.

With this principle in your mind, this principle of the flowing torrents of pure understanding which roll down and away the environments and possessions of men, you can see it is time someone spoke over the crossing and chaotic ideas of mankind, the absolute statements of Truth, and stopped describing the heterogeneous state of affairs formulated by foolish words spoken in hot moments. If, in volatile France, Voltaire's impetuous thoughts have been suddenly cut off by the statement that "Voltaire had no soul", so in plastic America your heartfelt *pronumdamento (proclamation),* hot from the splendor of Truth, may cause to dawn this day the fulfillment of prophecy which stops the slaying of animals for our clothing or food; stops the pain, the misery, which our preachers call the mystery of living; sets in order the Divine law of protection, providing, delighting, by the same quick demonstrations of understanding that Jesus Christ made. As atheism practically received its death-blow by a statement, so misery shall lie down in forgetfulness under your omnipotent word. What is misery but the fruit of a mistake figured out on the boards of life? If Truth is a river of cleansing, shall not the mistakes be clean washed off the world's life very easily? Does this seem reasonable to you? If it does, you have prepared the way for some demonstration of a new sort of good to come into your affairs. Just perceiving the reasonableness of Truth is all you have to do about it. Perception is demonstration. Hold steadily to your perception of the reasonableness of this doctrine whether you see it work out or not. It does its own work. It will work in unforeseen ways for your happiness. It will go speeding on to happily the lot of others.

The glory of this doctrine is that the instant you do truly perceive it you love it. You do not love it while you are studying the rules for thinking which lead up to the perception of it, but the clear light of the gospel is not possible to them that are not obedient unto the law. And the God who is neither law nor gospel, but is the Principle running through them, is not in you and visibly round you till you perceive reasonableness. The perception of reasonableness is God. So much Principle as you see the reasonableness of, so much God do you demonstrate, either immediately around you, or remotely from you, hastening now toward you.

September 25, 1892

LESSON II

ON THE HEALING OF SAUL

Acts 9:1-31

Swedenborg taught that the physical body is capable of being recuperated and cured of maladies by material means up to a certain point; beyond that point it must have spiritual food for renewal, and spiritual treatment for its cure, or fall under the death process.

Zoroaster (1200 B.C.) said, "One may heal with holiness, one may heal with law, one may heal with the knife, one may heal with herbs, one may heal with the Holy Word. Amongst all remedies, this is the healing one that heals with the Holy Word; this one is the best that will drive away sickness from the body of the faithful, for this one is the best healing of all remedies."

There are a great many invalids and sick people wandering up and down the earth for healing who will never be healed till they open their minds as docile little children to the Healing Word Zoroaster refers to.

Poor Saul of Tarsus needed healing of too much schooling, too much hearsay learning. He had swallowed every idea of God which his schoolmasters had given him, just as he had swallowed the Mishna and Gemara (they make up the Talmud), unquestioningly. So he wandered up and down seeking heretics to persecute, thinking to get his healing that way; but we know that it was the Truth, the Holy Word, he needed to restore his mind to the right state, just as we now know that people who have descended from chasers to heretics now need both bodily and mental healing by the right word.

"A right word, how good it is!" "Who can measure the force of a right word?" "He sent forth His Word and healed them."

There are millions of Sauls belonging to Brahminism, Buddhism, heathenism, and Christianism who, from hunting out heresies in their neighboring denominations, have now a great deal of trouble with their eyes, because such stupendous truths are now being proclaimed that their antique ideas fall flat when they esoterically meet them.

People who feel confident that what their parents and teachers told them about God's "mysterious" delighting in Jesus is true, have their confidence in a reed so brittle that when the wind of a Stephen's treatment strikes it they drop to the ground with eye troubles, rheumatic joints, quaking nerves. The only reason they do not know that it is their mental error meeting the spiritual truth of some illuminated mind is because they are not as good timbre as Saul. He was hardier, bolder, abler by nature than they, and hence had not been so enervated by his "much learning" as they are by theirs. He had more presence of mind to understand his emotions.

Oliver Wendell Holmes says that "the world's great men have not commonly been great scholars, nor its great scholars great men. The active mind feels itself above any and all human books." It is said of Whittier that if he had been a great scholar he would have enervated his genius. Not many minds are rugged enough in their natural genius to take too much *ipse dixii*. Saul, however, was one who had not been enfeebled by schooling; he had only become religiously knock-kneed, consequently he made a powerful opposition to the voice of the Absolute Truth when it struck his mind. He became totally blind.

At the present time, there are wonderful truths coming and going through the mental atmospheres, which act as treatments to the scholastic minds. If scholastic minds make powerful resistance they have powerful ailments. If they make pusillanimous objections, shying around the questions that arise, they have half-blind, half-deaf, half-enfeebled bodily states. All the ailments of intellectual people are due to their evading spiritual teachings.

There are prophecies in the earth that about this time many people shall suddenly fall by the wayside of human life; "the places that knew them once, shall know them no more forever." They shall disappear like shadows.

If spiritual truth is the substance, the intellect and flesh are shadows, when spiritual truth shines hot overhead why indeed should not the representatives of intellect and flesh disappear? Do not shadows always disappear at high noon? Saul could not be cured till a spiritually awakened member of the despised religious sect touched his blind eyes. Saul then became Paul the Apostle. Whoever yields to the irresistible truths of Spiritual Science becomes well aware that the spiritual intelligence of an Ananias is more capable than a Gamaliel to cure him of mental infirmity and physical disorder.

If, according to astrology, it was written that about this time you would die, you could not die in the old way if the living truth of Jesus Christ had appealed to your judgment. But you must make some change of mind and action as totally unlike your old self as if you had died. You do not disappear from the sight and sound of your former companions, maybe; and maybe you do; but you will make as definite a change of life and mind as Saul made by turning into Paul. The acceptance of a new line of reasoning changes your mind and life. You are dead to the former mind and life. If you have always been thinking that strong, bold, vigorous, active warfare against evil and wrong is the way to erase them from the human lot, and suddenly the illuminating text of the "Bhagavad-Gita" concerning the futility of active opposition to wrong and showing the more excellent way of Spirit, comes clear to you, those with whom you have worked will know you no more among them. They have not seen the Truth with you.

The full acceptance of the perfect truth would take us entirely out of the reach of our old methods. And it is the full acceptance of the Absolute Truth now by those who see that it is the Lord's second coming unto full salvation, which is putting as many as do receive it out of the reach of the old experiences and old methods.

To those who are afflicted with the disease of poverty, the perfect truth with respect to Jesus Christ comes with healing of poverty. If any of the agitators of these times think they are doing the Lord service by persecuting anyone of anything, they must be told that they are mistaken. If their methods are carried out, it would be only changing the money from a Rockefeller's hands to their hands, and we have abundant evidence that they do not understand finance. No; there is an acceptance of some spiritual propositions which would externalize as practically for the healing of poverty as Saul's blindness was healed.

It is the acceptance of some unwonted propositions which has healed thousands of men and women in later years of bodily infirmities. Half the time they did not know which proposition cured them. They cannot tell which proposition by their "not accepting" makes them continue miserable in certain other ways.

One has to accept certain truths for the cure of lameness, and other truths for the cure to shaking palsy. So one has to take certain ideas for the cure of timidity, and certain others for the cure of poverty, just as practically as the kitchen girl would use chalk for cleaning the silver and sand for the floor.

There was one who would not be healed of a particular kind of bodily sickness till she accepted the idea that Joshua caused the sun to seem to stand still, that Elisha multiplied the widow's oil, raised the Shunammite child to life, etc. Her belief in the limited action of Spirit was like a fence to hold in her malady.

Whatever the reason that makes you a machinist, with not wages enough to take care of your family, you may be sure it is not because you are not as capable as the neighbor who throws away more daily than you earn weekly, but because there is some one thing that you do not believe which you ought to believe. The instant you believe it, whatever it is, you will have some unexpected help from somewhere. Remember that any limitation is a disease. And take notice that poverty is a limitation as much as blindness or palsy.

The most cures of bodily disease have been made by calling them nothing but dreams; snubbing them as delusions. Poverty has usually declined to leave the premises by such a simple process as calling it a dream, snubbing it as nothing but a delusion. That disease has required some more metaphysical doctrines, as, for instance, that there is no God ruling over the world or over us; that all the God there is, is our own Spirit. We may be utterly astonished and as "struck down" as Saul when we first hear the idea; but if "Ananias" gives us the touch of his efficient explanations (or laying on of hands, as the ninth chapter of Acts calls it), we shall feel new power, new strength, new knowledge. It will be seen by us as a reasonable doctrine. Some people have to believe in symbols before they can be cured of the disease of ignorance. Symbols and signs and dreams and astrological foretellings are all perfectly accurate. They are not to be despised. See how much more Saul and Ananias knew after they had praised and believed in signs and dreams.

Do the stars then govern our destiny, according to Spiritual Science? No! We govern the stars and our destiny. The stars and the dreams are only innocent handwritings of our present status and our native possibilities. They are as truly nothing as the symbols of algebra. "The invisible things of God are clearly seen by the things that are made."

And these "made" things touch us for good at every turn. Generally we do not believe that dreams and stars tell us entirely of good. We believe they stand for evil, for dangers ahead, for deaths, for losses; but they forever prophesy of good only.

All the signals now thrown out concerning the speedy dissolution of this world and all things in it are signals of the great wave of spiritual understanding which shall touch the mind of man, now so diseased with mistaken statements of God, as Ananias touched Saul's eyes. There is a touching of the scales on the eyes of the world's theology which will make the end of Saul and give us Paul throughout all the earth. There is a touching of the scales on your mind which will snap or dissolve the filmy ideas which make you cringe before anyone or any situation in all the world, and show you wise as Socrates, Plato, Jesus. Perhaps you must say with vehemence, "It is not scholastic lore I need, it is to let my free Spirit speak it's 'I AM' in me and through me and by me."

Perhaps you are to speak forth the statement of pure metaphysics that, "It is not money I need, but to let the free Spirit within me claim its independence of matter, its independence of people, its independence of all things. The Spirit within is the Substance within. God is the only Substance. Shall God depend upon money, upon people, upon suitable circumstances to have all things, know all things, do all things? Neither then shall I depend upon any thing or circumstance, for the "'I AM' of me, the only 'I AM', is God".

Now this reasoning requires no exercise of the will. It simply requires your expression. The Physical Research Society, quite independent of the doctrine of Jesus, discovered that there is no need of exercising any will with our reasonings with people at a distance in order to make them respond, nor indeed with people near at hand. The reasonings accomplish their own meanings, as the words of Jesus Christ to the mind of Saul carried their own weight.

The Buddhists teach that four classes of people accomplish results with "righteous working" — which means right reasoning — viz., the afflicted, the searchers for truth, the poverty-stricken, and the wise.

The afflicted are sure to be relieved of their afflictions by talking to the inner nature which rests, so peaceful, within all bosoms forever. The restless wanderers of the earth, who are wondering always what is true among the multitudinous religions and philosophies (which amount to nothing as far as practical help goes) are sure to get convinced of what is true without a shade of doubt, if they address with praiseful words the wise inner nature forever resting so calm in their bosoms. The poverty-stricken come into their rightful inheritance if they speak to the all-holding Owner of worlds, forever resting so royally free within their own bosoms. The wise accomplish all things by describing face to face the Omniscience that sits as Omnipotent Principle forever within their own bosoms.

"Why, then, did the Buddhists not reap the fruits of such beautiful doctrine?" Because they never spoke truth to their own inner nature. They never practiced what they preached. Do you practice praising through the night watches while you are restlessly tossing with inability to sleep — praising and praising the Supreme Spirit resting within your own bosom? It was no more incumbent upon them to practice what they had heard of truth than it is upon you to do so.

Simple proclamations to the nature and place of the Spirit will cause the proclaimed results to come forth. Absolute Truth will bring absolute victory. Hear the Buddhists praising the Spirit within them for establishing caste, for distinguishing against women, for making certain animals more sacred than even their own children.

Is that absolute truth of the impartial, responding God?

Hear the Buddhists at their praises of the Spirit that dwells in their bosoms, telling it that it responds in their lives with exactly what they proclaim that it does, thus making themselves the arbiters of their own lot in life.

Hear the Christian at his devotions calling his God, a mystery. Hear him beg of a hard taskmaster to lessen the poverty, the suffering of his lot, fearing his God will not lessen it more than he believes that He will. Is that telling the Absolute Truth to the inner nature that waits in calm majesty the touch of your right words? Your own inner wisdom will not spring forth if you beg it to come. It will only stand out on the affairs of your life, on the health of your body, on the wisdom of your mind, by your describing it just as it is.

Zoroaster called the proclamation the Holy Word, the whole Truth. Of what do you need healing? Of the idea that you have had a hard life? Look, now, to the smiling majesty enthroned within you and tell it of its eternal peace. Do you need healing of sickness? Look now at the gracious Self dwelling in everlasting security within your own bosom, and tell it of its beautiful health.

Do you need healing of poverty, or of sorrow at the poverty of the world? Within your own bosom sits the Maker and Owner of all the universe. Is He poor? Is He in want? Is He mournful? Describe the greatness of that Center within you. As the sun breaks forth from the night, as he rides free on the highways of ether, so shall the sun of your world rise, so shall the scales of your night fall, so shall your mind ride free on the highways of the mistaken ideas of the world, and no man, no woman, no animal shall ever again cry under the dark doctrine of pain, of want, of ignorance, of loneliness, of bondage. Some of you cannot be absolutely healed till you hear the response, "I am God. There is no God." All is God. God is now free.

For this Being within hath a loud voice to touch you. Its Word is the holy healing of your world.

October 2, 1892

LESSON III

The Power of Mind Explained

Acts 9:32-43

Anaxagoras 500 B.C, finds the force which shapes the world, not in the nature of matter, nor in impersonal forces, but in a world-ordering Mind. This supreme Mind is distinguished from matter by simplicity, independence, knowledge, and supreme power.

Peter cured a "paralytic" and raised a "dead body" to life. It is evident he was not exercising the magnetic or mesmeric forces, for he explained that it was by the action of Jesus Christ the miracles were wrought, by the training potency of the words which represent the demonstrations of health and life. There has come up a revival of the idea of mental training by repeating words which concentrate many meanings in them. By repeating "Om" in various fashions the Brahmins said man would become God, for man would gradually appropriate an understanding of "OM" and understanding is God. With this understanding he should govern his world. And man is not truly appropriating of "Om" or Understanding, any more than he can demonstrate. This is the same as the saying of Jesus, *"If I do not the works of the Father, believe me not"*.

Spiritually we take from Spirit only what we are willing to give forth. The prayer, *"Forgive us our debts as we forgive our debtors"*, means that we cannot take any more forgiveness than we can give forth. The same with mercy. The same with friendship. The same with all good. No one is realizing or enjoying a moiety (portion) more than he is bestowing.

There is but one lake on the surface of the globe that has no outlet, and that is the Dead Sea. All of us belong in mental geography to some material country or sea, which is more typical of us than any other country or sea. Those who are choosing not to give forth of their mental riches belong to the Dead Sea type. To give forth our mental riches is to be speaking and thinking what the Spirit is doing; not mentioning what the flesh is doing. "The flesh profiteth nothing."

Dorcas had been thinking of the kindness of God till her hands had wrought many great deeds. Peter had been thinking of the Life of God till his voice could raise the dead. Aeneas had been thinking of the unexpected actions of God in miracles till be sprang up from palsy, because another, who also believed in miracles, spoke suddenly to him. Two people together visiting at our house, both strong in confidence that our prayers will be answered, will quicken our spiritual faculties to lay hold of the blessings we are seeking. On the same principle two visitors, strongly intellectual believers that we are very foolish to trust so much to aid from miraculous sources, will chill the atmosphere and discourage us mentally till we begin ourselves to doubt. This will make a delay in the answers to our prayers. What kind of people are near you — those of simple confidence in miracles, or those who consider all expectations of incalculable interpositions in your behalf folly? You may compute your depressions or exalted hopes from the mental radius of such people as are your companions.

Peter was an uplifting visitor wherever he went. All believers in the power of Mind welcomed him with delight. He meditated so much on the visibility of God through repeating the Name Jesus Christ that miracles always accompanied him. Something always transpires wherever we go which is of the nature of our persistent feelings before we arrive there. Peter cured Aeneas and aroused Dorcas according to this lesson. He had taken his mind off the external persecutions of the young church so long that he was in an exalted state of mind, just suited to heal. People, who are thinking of how badly they are used, or how badly someone is acting, do not carry enlivening atmospheres with them. The persecutions of the church were suspended, about long enough before Peter went down to Lydda to give his buoyant mind time to quicken with extra ozone through breathing and eating and drinking two glorifying words. He told Aeneas that those two words were the healing force working instantaneously with him. "And Peter said unto him, Aeneas, Jesus Christ maketh thee whole: arise, and make thy bed. And he arose immediately." The two words always come to fruitage exactly the moment our type of mind gives forth its confidence, its love, its expectation to them.

Aeneas believed in miracles, but he did not believe it was quite time he himself received one, did not think himself quite ready for one to take place for his own benefit. Peter was the very opposite. With Peter everything was NOW. His belief in the "now" of the miracle struck down the "by and by" of the paralytic's mind, and up he stood whole. The entire battle of mind, one the "by and by" kind, and the other the "now" kind showed forth. All battles are in the mental before the externals figure them out. One idea in everyone always yields to some idea in every other mind it meets. Some outside movement will indicate it. You believed James was in the wrong till you met Thomas and talked with him about the Presidential campaign. You never mentioned James, but you go home in certainty that James is right. This is because Thomas understands the truth of the case. Your idea is eliminated, beaten out, by Thomas's understanding. No words spoken aloud, no special thoughts on the subject are necessary. Every change of sentiment, every new manner of looking at a question, results from someone's understanding, the true inwardness of the question. If you are a procrastinator like Aeneas, get somewhere near impetuous people who never can wait a moment for anything. If they believe in miracles you will find yourself dispatching your work with miraculous speed.

Similarly, if you are one who belongs to the multitude of those who tell what good works used to be done, either by the apostles or in the early day of the faith cures of Spiritual Science, you need to have a Peter type of mind come visiting you at "Joppa". It is death, or old age, to talk of what used to be so much better than is now. Peter, the impetuous "Now", puts every idea of the past out of your house and makes his own prompt action startle your shrinking wish into exhibition. Peter himself is not more eager for great miracles of cure than procrastinators and backward lookers are, but he believes in expedition. Peter was the idea of instantaneousness which Jesus left to walk visibly when He thought it expedient that He go away. The idea still remains, though Peter, its representative, himself has gone away. We find this idea of the dead being raised to life, as Tabitha was in this ninth chapter of Acts, and of Aeneas being healed, instantly, always exhibited by the effect of certain people's mental presence among us. If they are utterly given up to the idea they do strong works promptly. If they take the idea faintly they do not do mighty things promptly, but simple works, like cheering people quickly, or giving excellent judgments without waiting to think. Only intense confidence wakes a man out of paralysis and a woman out of death.

The mind that raises the dead to life with a few words, and quickens palsied limbs with a sentence is the one that is all given up to what already is. It does not talk to you about "growth" and "evolution". Those words get utterly routed when the true Peter-mind saying, "There is no time in Spirit, no growth or progress in Spirit all is now," comes near.

Aeneas represents one who thinks of what great things are going to be done. This is palsy. Dorcas and her friends represent those who rehearse what great things have already been done. This is death. Peter represents one who sees life and accomplishments, as neither past nor future, but now.

The body is not the only thing that gets palsy by looking forward. Knowledge, ability along any chosen line, stops, paralyzed with the idea that some time we will attempt the work we see ought to be done. Be bold to believe that today is the day meant for your healing, your stirring prosperity along some line.

"Boldness hath genius, power, and magic in it.
What you can do or dream you can, begin it!"

The body is not the only thing that acts out deadness by looking backward over what used to be done. The enterprises you ought to be engaged in this moment, which were intended for your quickening delight and unalloyed success, will have nothing interesting or stirring in them when you think of them if you talk much of the past. It is as bad for the mind to contemplate the past as it is to anticipate the future even worse, if this lesson is taken literally. All is mind. You will see plenty of charm in enterprises if you never remember the good old times nor hope for better times. Refuse to meditate an instant on what has been or what shall be. Just this minute is the minute everything is alive, healthy, strong, successful with you in Spirit. You can demonstrate as much "present" as you appropriate the idea of — as you let of Peter into your "house" — into "Joppa". They could not do anything with only a part of Peter in their cities — that is, with descriptions of him. That means we have to have the idea of "now" get complete possession of our premises.

How shall we do this? Peter did it by repeating the Name Jesus Christ over and over. Those two words usually hurry a man or woman over a whole lifetime of experiences within a short time.

The speaking of the word "now" has prompt efficiency with some people. It is not superstition; it is as sensible for mind to hold, by repeating over and over, certain words, as it is for the outward body to eat oatmeal. One feeds the mind and the other symbolizes feeding the mind. Aeneas had mental starvation. A few words refreshed him.

Dorcas had mental exhaustion. A few words revived her.

Peter was so pleased with the natural result of keeping the idea that Jesus Christ is now working, healing, and encouraging among us, that he concluded to stay in that state of mind, so he abode many days in it. This indicates that if you have an exalted certainty of the healing and quickening power this instant you may keep it intensifying with happiness as long as you please. That gleam of glad recognition of your own spiritual nature will be your constant home of bright rest by your saying, "I will abide here forever".

People should not say that "they were at one time in just the right state of mind to do great works, but do not feel equal to them now". The name of the Good is "I am". It is the Free Masons who have changed the statement of Being from "I am that I am" to "I was, but am no more". If they had kept the teachings of Moses, while letting his mighty inner voice proclaim itself, they might have had every sign of the presence and working of good among us which we are asking for. The new Free Masons, now reviving the Spirit of Christ, do not say that they "were" strong, they "were" wise, they "were" rich, they "were" happy. They know very well that to be telling of the past is cold death. Notice how cold and dead Dorcas was to those who thought of what activities she used to exhibit; so even the most inviting prospect in our affairs will seem to have no life, no substance, no goodness in it for you who keep talking of "I was, but now am not as strong as I would like to be or as well, as wise, as satisfied".

To look forward is paralysis. To look backward is death. The name of the good in us ready to demonstrate with the world of affairs is "I Am".

After we have settled the question of "now" we may say "I was". Being confident of today we may speak of "I will be". The Good lies back of us — "I am Alpha". The Good lies ahead of us — "I am Omega". The Good is now here.

Peter showed forth another important principle, that is, we are not to be mindful of praise or blame if we would do our most enlivening works. Peter was indifferent to blame, Dorcas was dead to praise. This combination wrought a miracle. We are not to swerve to the right for blame, nor to the left for praise. Keep your mind's eye on your own business and have as little as possible to do with the opinions of people.

Still another fact comes to light in the ethics of life from Peter's conduct as set forth in this lesson, namely, do not attempt to fight for your reputation or character. Be above reputation, above concern therefore. If Peter had failed to bring Tabitha into manifest life he would have had the reputation of proclaiming a science he could not demonstrate. It would seem as if he were filled with vanity to even attempt to do the works of Jesus — to even say they ought to be done. He did not care what he might seem to be; his whole concern was with the duty that lay before him. He practiced his Science on every situation, regardless of appearances.

Lastly, we see by this lesson that Peter had the solution to the ancient question of "how to animate the particular from the universal". Every "particular", which means every single manifested thing, can receive unlimited renewal, infinite reanimation, from the universal, by the absorption of the kind of living fire which get kindled by independence of mind in regard to spiritual matters. If you perceive that "Simon the Tanner" is a spiritually awakening companion, commune with him often, be comrade with him much, though the church and your social acquaintances object. To be in the right and know it, with "Simon the Tanner", is better than to be pampered by opposing princes. Be comrades with the spiritually-minded that you may be a better minister to the unspiritual.

October 9, 1892

LESSON IV

FAITH IN GOOD TO COME

Acts 10:1-20

Cornelius and Peter magnified every sign and vision and dream that came to them as signifying some new power for good. Abraham was noted for believing every symbol to be the intention of some great good for him. Believing so innocently in the good, sure enough, each prognostication turned to their advantage eventually, no matter through what seas and winds of trial it steered its way to reach them. Cornelius gave "much alms and prayed God always". Peter had regular hours of each day set apart to prayer.

The true prayer is affirmation. The true almsgiving is denial. We hear of thousands upon thousands of worthy people asking assistance from rich church members, but not getting it, because the good, kind church people do not realize the difference between where and where not to bestow their bounty. They hide discernment, they show no judgment.

A systematic course of affirmation and denial, or speaking truth from both positive and negative, such as is mentioned in our present lesson, the tenth chapter of Acts, would uncover their judgment and quicken their discernment. The power of discernment and strength of right judgment belong to all men and all women and all living creatures in exactly the same quantity and quality. Every man is as divine as Jesus Christ. The only possible distinction between any man, no matter what is his calling or seeming character, and Jesus, is that Jesus Christ told of His divinity and yielded Himself to His words, while the rest of mankind, even if they proclaim their divinity, do not yield to their words.

The measure of casting one's self into one's words is the measure of that person's demonstration of divinity. Abraham kept to the saying that was constantly in his mouth — *"The Word of the Lord"*. Every thing that came to pass with him or came near him he was sure was the "Word of the Lord". No matter through what seas of experience we pass after having an uplifted sense of the action of an unusual phenomenon in our lives, we are to see by faith some great good to come. It is sure to arrive. A right practice of keeping to this speaking of our divinity and casting ourselves into our words would make us demonstrate all of our divinity as Jesus demonstrated all of His. Then, like Cornelius, we would bestow our alms wisely and our prayers would be availing.

Outward wise almsgiving is the symbol of right denial. The right denial for want, hunger, need, beggary, is, "There is no want, no hunger, no need, no beggary". This is speaking Truth from the negative. Then the hands will make haste to act in such a fashion that those words will be proven all around in our world. There will be shown to be no want, no beggary, no lack. What the mouth speaketh, the world shall make visible. A metaphysician who had some secret doctrine taught that the Light of the world is within us all, and if we cannot perceive the Light within ourselves we cannot perceive it anywhere. The voice that spoke to Moses was his own interior voice. It sometimes reflected itself upon the external atmosphere, but it was his own Spiritual voice. Our voice of the Spirit may seem to speak from without, but forever it is the Warrior within, the Light within, the Voice within, escaping forth when we know what is true, or when we see a vision with a warning, or hear a voice with a message.

Thus if we stop to argue against it we make a conflict within ourselves which is as sure to show forth in outward events as Peter's arguments against his own Spiritual judgment showed forth in the opposition of his Christian colleagues. Peter finally yielded to the spiritual voice that broke forth from his mind and reflected itself on the airs around him; so also finally the Christians who opposed him yielded to his judgment. No argument worth giving voice to can be brought up when a spiritual principle is announced.

What possible worth is there in an argument for the reality of crime. Is it an argument for its reality that we claim to see it with our eyes and hear it with our ears?

What use is there in such an argument as that, when every identical thing we see with our eyes, hear with our ears, feel with our sentiments, is the formulation of a belief?

Why do we need to believe in such things as if they were real when our belief is entirely within our control? Shall we not believe what we please? And shall we not please to believe what stands to reason? From time to time there have been strong, wise reasoners trying to show that all external things are dependent utterly on man's ideas. Aristotle, Descartes, Berkeley, Collier — read over their writings and see what brave struggles they made to disentangle the mind of man from the network of belief in outward and seeing phenomena as having any controlling efficiency further than mind itself has given them.

One moment Peter showed confidence in the voice of his Spirit, the next he reverted to his old prejudices. "A house divided against itself cannot stand." Have we not all believed one way one moment and another way the next? Have we not, therefore, tangled and mixed environments? How do we know what sort of affairs would surround us if we were to believe one way constantly?

In our lesson it speaks of the ninth hour and the sixth hour. The ninth hour is three o'clock in the afternoon, and the sixth hour is twelve o'clock in the morning. In mental training they are important hours in the day. One is for withdrawing accusations from the world and from ourselves, and the other is for making the affirmation we would see soonest demonstrated. At three o'clock Cornelius felt his prayers and alms taking effect before his very eyes. There are times when Spiritual ideas that have been held in mind are seen plainly to be coming into manifestation. He heard a voice announcing that what he had been thinking and Speaking had come up as flowers in the sunshine of the presence of God. He teaches us patience, persistence, and presence of mind. When it comes to a time when all things respond to our ideas we do not dictate to them, we listen to them.

There is a law by which things work exactly according to our ideas, as there is a law by which roses bloom according to their climate. Ideas in your home make a climate in which things and affairs spring up. A family always denying that they can afford this and that will fix their business affairs so that it will some time be very apparent that they cannot have anything. A family always fearing for the children's health will fix one of them to be a chronic invalid early or late in life. Yet the invalidism and the lack will not be real; they will simply represent the ideas of those who worried so much. This principle being known, we see how great a practice it would be for us to stop, like Cornelius, from having any ideas at all for a while every day. It would give us a great rest, and as ideas fall down at once into the sands at our feet when we let go of them, we shall thus leave our Spiritual "self" free to see and hear things from its own standpoint. There will be no more puzzling over books on language, no more worrying over mathematical computations of how to make both ends meet, no more scrambling and struggling for place and power, no more competition. The divine "Ego", being uncovered of the ideas that we must go through these things, will calmly tell the universe, as the maker of languages, the origin of numbers, the owner of its world, that it was only the illusion of the "what might be if it were not free", which has circles around mankind.

Cornelius loved the fruits of his ideas. People who complain are only whimpering because they do not like the fruits of their ideas. As it is good for ground to lie untilled for a space, so it is good for our world if we do not forevermore plow it with our ideas, harrow it with our notions, enrich it with our erudition concerning the nature of evil, the origin of religion, the history of Rome, the marbles of Phidias, the statistics of crime; nor sow it with seeds of new science, new policy, new inventions, all relating to total unrealities. Peter did not love and he did love, all in a minute, the fruits of his past ideas. He should have kept silent when he was faced by the net full of creeping and crawling creatures. We will not think anything. Then they will fall away, leaving only the sight of spiritual kindness, giving us freely the sound of love at every turn, feeding us, prophesying for us.

Peter had no cause to dispute that what was spread for him to eat was good, only such cause as he had learned independent of spiritual judgment. We have no cause to see evil in our world, only such cause as we have chosen to believe exists unlike supreme goodness. It will be a great rest for us to cease believing contrary to what is true. It will spread our table with bread and milk and honey to cease from thinking at all, while the living Spirit is working out our provisions, our wisdom, our actions for us. It may seem to the world that we are thinking and working, but indeed Spirit is responsible when we choose to cease from imaginations. "The Father that dwelleth within us doeth the work."

October 16, 1892

LESSON V

EMERSON'S GREAT TASK

Acts 10:30-48

Emerson teaches that the gods always overload with disadvantages those whom they have appointed to great tasks. Homer must be blind; Virgil must have asthma; Epictetus must be a deformed field slave. As Emerson had been appointed by the gods to a greater task than any he had in mind, he was more overloaded than any, for it cometh unto a man that what he really believeth, what he really convenanteth with as a principle, will work out with him.

Peter had been really preaching that God is no respecter of persons, so he was faced up with the compulsory companionship of people with whom it was an "unlawful thing", according to Jewish creed, to "keep company", no matter how good they might be. Had Peter refused to stand by his preaching when this demand for a demonstration met him he would have been defeated in his later conferences with the Christianized Jews. Many of us can attribute our misfortunes and failures to our once having refused to stand up to our ideas when they confronted us with their situations. As Peter stood to the practicalization of his religion, he won by his arguments when the Christians got to quarreling. Moses taught this idea to Esdras by a figure of speech, *"Let the waters bring forth."* Surely the conscious words and thoughts we speak do bring forth. And there is no principle we can fellowship with which hurries us into its situations like a high and lofty religious sentiment.

The greatest miracles on record have been wrought by highly religious people. Religious principle acts like a hot sunshine over the waters or flowing ideas of our minds, and warms and vitalizes them so that they bleed with life at every point where we cut them. Our words are alive.

Any principle held as the light or guide of our life will, by and by, vitalize our words with its purport. Klopstock was waited upon by some musicians, from Gottingen, who travelled to Hamburg, to ask what he meant by a certain passage in "The Messiah."

"I do not this moment recollect what I did mean," he said, "but it would pay you, gentlemen, to devote your life to finding out what I meant." He had such living, practical confidence in his principle that, being one with it, he knew that what it said through him was right.

Hannibal "swore eternal hate to Rome" as a boy, and lived and taught that hate principle so constantly that the sound of his voice was a terror to his foes. Hannibal is at the gates, was the synonym for "destruction is nigh".

When a high religious proposition strikes the mind and becomes its daily theme for years all the words brought forth in relation to it live and act. If you were to set up an imagination of a perfect human body in your mind and describe that continually you would make healthy bodies appear near you for a long time, but as it would be an imagination of a form or symbol it would fail you sometime. The enduring and increasing power is our religious reasoning.

The twelve propositions of Spiritual Science are the highest religious reasonings. They have perfectly shining meanings lying just back of the outer wordings of them. It has been found that whoever penetrates these outer wordings and sees, hears, smells, tastes, feels, knows the splendid intentions of them, finds his outer eyesight and his hearing and knowing faculties sharpened and quickened. It has also been found that it is a stubborn stopping short of penetrating into the meanings of things which causes a loss of the faculties in so many people.

If we do not want our religious ideas to work freely with us we have thrown up hard barriers of refusals. If you are wondering why your high religious ideas do not carry you more safely over the trials of your lot, you will find it is simply because you let your mind descend from its lofty reasonings to describe material performances.

Michelangelo would not allow himself to discuss the faults of other artists. He shut himself alone with his own lofty ideals, and so kept his mind in a high altitude all the time. This caused itself to express what belonged to it perfectly. If you have a leaning to some special line of art, increase and improve your ideals of it. Do not discuss the opposition of it at all. The belt of your planet is small very small — if you stop from talking ideals to discuss imperfect works. A critic always has a small belt to his sphere. A critic is always a small mind. For one who is in the daylight of his art while he is thinking ideals, is in the night time while he is thinking of poor works. So if he turns from the perfect to the imperfect quickly his planet must turn quickly on its axis. Look out for the highest along your own line.

> "One science only will one genius fit.
> So vast is art, so narrow human wit."

Keep your mind on ideals. This continual flow of the river of thought will bring forth fruits at every turn. Let it do so. Peter here preached Jesus Christ so eloquently to the audience of people he once would have shrunk from, that it has become a living and active Christian idea that there are no high nor low in Christ. All are equally endowed; all have the same opportunities to perfect themselves in their art, whatever it may be, by keeping the highest ideals in mind, by making idealism their religion. And the highest idealism is religion, no matter what you are studying. Its highest swing is Jesus Christ, or the expression of soul. In the practice of Christian healing we do not setup an image within our mind, and we do not imagine how a perfect man or woman would look; we keep reasoning onward along the lines of what God thinks. Like Kepler we say often, "O, God! I think Thy thoughts after Thee." At every turn, this way of thinking breaks forth into demonstration.

If we descend from our upper stratum of reasoning to discuss the faults and foibles of human beings we are astonished to see how chilled we get with the disappointments of people not being cured, helped, comforted by our high line of thought. We are apt to think the high lines are not demonstrable.

John the Revelator speaks of four themes which cause the mind's descent so that high demonstrations do not appear. Jesus speaks of our never discussing certain subjects if we would keep the mind swinging on the axis of eternal day. We must not talk about what it is healthy or unhealthy, expensive or cheap to eat; nor discuss what we ought or ought not to wear; nor confer with each other about what is safe or unsafe, good or wicked to drink. We may speak of the doctrine that heals, cleanses, quickens, and comforts. Doctrine is the only safe theme.

John the Revelator says that if we do not bring out the perfections of health, wisdom, peace, in everyone we meet, it is because we have stopped to talk about or think about one of four things. One of these things that the mind must forever be above is thinking that we ourselves, or any other living creature, have appetites or passions lower than the breathings of the Holy Ghost. He who preaches Jesus Christ must hold forever that no man of flesh is our father. God alone brought us forth. Do not descend to talk of heredity of appetites or association with temptations if you would make your words vascular at every point where the demonstration of purity is called for.

Another topic that the mind is not to descend into thinking or the voice into speaking about, is that there is anything against anyone or anything. Whoever says opium is dangerous, or distillations of cereals or compositions of minerals are offensive, is descending from the ideal reasonings of God, who pronounced all things good. No one shall speak against the climate, the draughts, the actions of earth's creatures, for he who would see them good must think along the thoughts of God. We shall not permit the lowering of the mind's holy reasonings into the thought of the talk of sin in the world or in ourselves. Sin is not a theme we can give any thought to. Many a good reasoner in Science wonders why his thoughts do not live and thrive at the harbors of demonstration where he halted them. He may remember that yesterday or last week he descended into the idea of the selfishness of Mary, or the jealousy of James, or his own temper gave him regret. A fall of the barometer of reasoning must chill the delicate process of demonstration.

Peter here keeps up his majestic thoughts of the wisdom of God as pouring through all mankind, and permits not his mind to linger in the suggestion of how differently he had formerly believed. This stately march of thought suddenly breaks forth in the audience. "The Holy Ghost fell on all those which had the word." By this uplifted sweep of the Science shall the Holy Ghost fall upon this whole world.

The African Princes shall lift up their hands from slaughter, for there is a reasoning driving over the planet from the mind of the changeless God. Asia shall feel the shadow of her long belief in a karma folded around her ignorance, flee away into the infinite day of pure knowledge as God thinks of His people. Europe shall let go her clutch on the masses through keeping them in poverty, for a high tide of Spiritual feeling is being driven over her shores by the sunlight of a pure and undefiled doctrine, away out of the jurisdiction of the church that has stopped on the line of her march of teaching the everlasting protection of God to teach that He also calls some to misery. America shall cease from her mad scrambles for gold, for her mind shall catch the secret gleam of a Light that is shining from a people as inspired as Peter, with the certainty that undefiled Science will feed and clothe and heal without traffic or competition of man with man.

"The Lord shall suddenly come to His temple." The God whom ye have covenanted with shall write upon the bells of the horses, "Holiness", and upon the hearts of the world, "Peace". If ye have covenanted with hate ye shall have a name that shall strike terror like Hannibal; if ye have covenanted with love ye shall have the healed world for the signal of your chosen principle; if ye have covenanted with the principle of the absolute equality of all men in rights of possessions, happiness, wisdom, like Peter, be sure that the messenger of the covenant, whom ye delight in, shall come suddenly, and the gift of the unstinted Presence of God shall be demonstrated in the happy and wise earth which prophecy has prepared for this age.

In Spiritual Science there is no covenant with hate. The love of God is her only theme. Make your covenant now with love.

October 23, 1892

LESSON VI

THE TEACHING OF FREEDOM

Acts 11:19-30

As lions crouch on their haunches and rally with mighty skill all the living forces concealed within them, to spring far and hard, so the Christian Jews rehearsed the prophesies of the Messiah to come, and preached that Jesus had fulfilled them till their confidence was generated to the point of irresistible oratory.

Emerson tells us it is the man drunk with conviction who convinces. The early Christian apostles were drunk with conviction. They rallied their conviction by constant repetition of their reasons for believing that Jesus was Christ. For a long time they, as a body of Jew Christians, rehearsed their reasonings among themselves. Then the fires of their religion broke out and they told the twelve points of Christian doctrine to the outside world. As the trained ranger over Texan plains lassoes the wild steer, so the trained Christian thinkers added a multitude of believers to their incontrovertible principles.

Every separate statement of Bible history is the Rosetta stone to the solution of an individual problem, a national situation, a church state of affairs. As the masterly reasonings and transcendent religious sentiments of prehistoric Egypt lay like a sealed book under moonless night to the early Greek scholar, the Roman priest, the Oriental traveler, the German, French, English savant, till Champollion threw the light of wise interpretation over the hieroglyphics of the Rosetta stone, so have lain the Acts of the Apostles under the cloudy materialism of modern interpretation till Spiritual Science threw the ray of her twelve-pointed star of revelation over them. Hereby we learn to interpret what made the Christians of Apostolic times so efficient in converting to accord with their ideas. Hereby we learn how by constant thought upon the oneness of man with God in Substance, Wisdom, Power, the young Jesus of Nazareth suddenly broke loose from His human nature, which works no miracles, and became in demonstration divine nature which works miracles.

At Cana of Galilee Jesus made the silent proclamation of His marriage with God and transformed the six stone water pots to tankards of red reviving wines. Under the light of the morning star of the science of Christ we read that so His doctrine milled in the heart shall transform the six homely circumstances of every human lot into the red wine of beautiful associations. In the desert place Jesus increased five loaves and two fishes to abundant provision for five thousand men, besides women and children, by blessing and praising the meager supply. The new radiance of the revival of His thoughts in pure metaphysic tells us that we also in the seeming desert of our cheerless life may take the few little possessions we do have, whose meagerness has so long offended us, and praise and bless them till they multiply into new treasures straight from the bounty of the ever-willing law of praise.

At the grave of Lazarus He thanked the Lifeforce that it had a law whereby if He spoke boldly forth the command of His soul, His command would be obeyed by the breaking forth of the Lifeforce in the dead and buried Lazarus. By the light of His love I read my story as it lies here at my feet. I see, as the glory of His intention strikes my understanding, that when grief or resentment holds my whole being in its intense throes, that then is the supreme moment for me to decree a thing and it shall be established unto me, "Come forth, divine healing power!"

In this eleventh chapter of Acts, beginning at verse nineteen, we see that there shall spring a moment over the entire earth when all the people shall see that the light in all mankind is One. The prophecy of the great white rose of spiritual blooming shall be fulfilled. *"And in the days of these kings shall the God of Heaven set up a Kingdom which shall never be destroyed; and the Kingdom shall be left to other people, but it shall break in pieces and consume all the other kingdoms, and it shall stand forever."*

This everlasting Kingdom is the teaching of Spirit that there is no need to teach children not to tell lies, for if they know what the Spirit in them is speaking they cannot lie. There is no need to teach men not to overreach, for with the spoken words of the Apostles of Jesus the Light that now lights every man shall flame forth with the Holy Ghost of love and mercy. As the early Apostles showed how the carpenter's Son, by speaking forth to the world His inner knowledge, shone with Christ, so apostles of today declare that by speaking forth the same Mind that was in Jesus, all men can shine with Christ.

This Kingdom is the teaching of freedom. There is a transcendent freedom awaiting the people. The Apostles threw off the yoke of caste ideas and breathed the breath of the knowledge that there is no man, no woman, no child less than Christ. This free air gave them new healing powers, new providing energies. They were able to send food in the days of famine to far-off people. But they still held themselves under the yoke of expectation of martyrdom; they still held themselves under the fear that some of their members might speak too freely of the freedom of God.

Martin Luther rose up from the slippery staircase of belief that good works will open the spiritual nature to heavenly powers, to the more upright position that "the just shall live by faith". He breathed the air of a new freedom. But he still held the idea that no one could be saved into spiritual airs except by obeying his dogma. When the still freer doctrine that man is greater than his dogmas was offered him, he closed down on the opening rose of his opportunity and refused the loving Melanchthon's eternal friendship, because he had not yet accepted his ideas. He had not been staunch to confidence in his ideas as right. He had made himself free by them; but man's freedom for himself to worship God after the light of his own mind may take the swing that others must see as he does or die.

The great Chrysostom could answer like the free Christ that they could not exile him, for God was his home; they could not defraud him, for his treasures were in heaven; they could not defame him, for his witness was in heaven and his record was on high. But he chained himself from a new freedom by being among those early church fathers who believed in the subjection of women and abject obedience to the rod for little children.

See the wondrous glory that shone over the multitude at the free utterance of these preachers at Antioch! Their voices stirred the proud city to name them by the divinest Name that the planet ever quivered under. See them close down on the opening rose of opportunity after opportunity to show themselves in full fellowship with the absolutely free Jesus. Why did they expect martyrdoms and imprisonments? Though Agabus prophesied famine, should they meekly agree with him, with the example of the blasting of the fig tree still pictured in memory? Had they not heard that Christ opened prison doors to set captives free, not to receive them? Had they not heard that Christ is Truth? Could they not gather from the coming and going of the risen Christ that they need not die to reach heaven, that they need not preach regulations about eating or clothing, for the Spirit should clothe and feed wisely?

When they spoke of being transformed by renewing of the Mind, having the same Mind in them which was in Christ Jesus, need they have refused the next teaching of the over-beaming sunshine of truth, that all Spirit is God; powerful to close down on the schools, the churches, the kingdoms which tell that some are inferior, some superior, some clothed and some needing clothes?

To this day their idea of waiting to go through the tomb to be in Heaven has held the church from the bloom of life; but the Truth is not that we wait for our life of immunity from pain and trouble. The Truth is that we as Spirit are above the necessity for time. As Spirit, we do not stop amid the clashing ways of mortality. We rise out of them now. Their idea to which they were chained has come down over the centuries to us and held us as a

Christianized people in its folds, that we must send missionaries and alms to the benighted and hungry part of God's Presence. The Science of Christ understood tells that abiding at home, the Spirit of man may speak to the Spirit of man and there shall be food and raiment come folding the people with gladness.

Does such a message from the Spirit within us, speaking that which is true of Spirit, stop the sending of ships to the Blacks of the islands and books to the heathen of India? It will work out to the sight of the mind a new consciousness, an understanding why the far races beg us to send truth and not run to their shores.

We have no right to speak of the darkness of mind of races stepping on the planet of God. The Light that lighteth every man lighteth them also. We have no right to speak of the hunger and sadness of children walking over the plains of the earth of our God.

As sickness cannot be found when we proclaim from the Spirit that it is absent, so ignorance cannot be found on the glove when you sail around her God-protected belts. Go with the gospel that man is all-wise with the wisdom of God and you will not find a Black man eating his neighbor or hurting his children.

"Seek Me and ye shall find Me." Go seek God in the wilds of Africa and see Jesus Christ smiling with infinite beauty, unlimited wisdom, from every face you meet "Is this practical," you ask, "with the

reports of the Livingstones and Stanleys of civilization explaining the darkness and sadness of Africa?" Just as you have now received the doctrine that sickness and bodily pain are not here, but only an imaging forth of what we have supposed, so there is no need of missionaries, no need of books, for ignorance, savagery, race distinctions are only the mirage of our supposition. Seek wisdom on the islands and find wisdom. Seek the splendor of judgment and the knowledge of all the ages focused into all and each of living creatures, and find them.

This is the kingdom that shall come to the earth in the days of the kingship of scholarship which believes in ignorance, of government which believes in inferior and superior, of church which believes in imperfection. Enlarge the bounds of your ministry. Open the expectation of your mind. As true as there is no sickness, so true is it there is no poverty, no ignorance.

Shall there be an end of such a doctrine as this? Is it not what God says of His Kingdom? Shall I dare tell what God does not tell? This doctrine is Jesus come waking us up in our home. It shall stand forever.

October 30, 1892

LESSON VII

SEEK AND YE SHALL FIND

Acts 12:1-17

People seem to be all seeking something. They take a multitude of ways to arrive at the object of their restless search. It is written: *"Seek and ye shall find."* So the good or satisfaction people are seeking they will come at without doubt. Some things people get right away on this plane of existence, called mortal. Other things people wait for the astral plane to fulfill.

Herod loved to "please" the majority vote. So he beheaded everyone that those in power of public opinion wanted him to. Peter loved to do things which he thought would please one man. So he kept courting martyrdoms and imprisonments. They had very rough ideas of ways and methods for bringing about a satisfied state of mind, but hardly more rough than the ideas people nowadays have who imagine that it pleases Jesus Christ for them to tell that the Christian walk is one of hardship and suffering.

It is related of a soldier in the East Indies that his comrades threw a basin of soup into his bosom to test his patience after his conversion to Christianity. He had been a prize-fighter, and they hoped he would fight at this insult. He, however, looked up calmly and said, "This is what I must expect if I become a Christian." Well, who taught him to "seek and find" such things as that? Was he not rather bending like a reed under the wind of a popular opinion of the Christian walk than standing straight up like a pillar of faith with the early proclamation, "I do not believe in violence and hardship"? "They that seek Me early shall find Me." Who is this "Me" the soldier might have found? "The Prince of Peace." He had a right to the peace of God. Does God suffer? Then remember it is not Godlike to suffer. Those who are most like God suffer least.

People imagine it is very pleasing to God for them to tell how ignorant they are. Is God ignorant? Did He have an ignorant mind out of which to form part of His children? Is He not our Father? Did not His hand fashion us? Out of His own Substance created He not us? Is not that a rough idea of what is pleasing to the Infinite Wisdom who "fashioned all hearts alike"? Some imagine that it pleases God for them to be sick, lame, poverty-stricken. Did God have a portion of His Being sick, lame, poverty-stricken, out of which to make these people?

Even with a few of these notions lugging along in your mind, it is amazing how grandly one little ray of truth given forth will work. Pastor Harms, of the Hanover Mission, did not believe in begging. He did believe in getting money by the Spirit of God. So he told the Spirit daily how good It was to him and let such a warm stream of gratitude run free over the universe that it attracted to him in one year $14,781. No one had bent him to the notion that a Christian ought to go half naked and hungry, but he did yield to a point on the "barely enough" idea, for he felt it was a "skin of the teeth" getting through, that after all his prayers he had only $15 over his expenses. He would not let the full doctrine of "abundance" flow through him.

Peter, in this twelfth chapter of Acts, had evidently let the protecting idea flow freely enough — so that it was only reined in by his seeking a crucifixion later on. "Not yet", was his constant idea concerning his own cross. Some of us hold the "not yet" for our benefits. We are all seeking our good. According to the law we shall find it. As it is meant for us, let us put out our hands and take it as Peter took the angel's word and got out of prison. We have great wisdom belonging to us particularly; by putting out our hands — right ideas — we shall show forth this wisdom, must put the right ideas to it unceasingly, as it is written the Church did for Peter that he might be set free. To the radiance of your own wisdom speak truly how strong it is, how efficient it is, how beautiful it is. You will get out of this prison house of your imagination that to shut wisdom back is pleasing to the Divine Wisdom, or makes you more companionable to your friends, or is of any present or future advantage to yourself.

You have a hidden Peter, a hidden healing power. Be a Church praying without ceasing for the freedom of that healing power. Tell it how quick it is in action, how sure it is to touch the right case, how willing to speed with strength every instant. Our lesson tells that as soon as the angel had wrought the miracle of delivering Peter out of prison he "departed". Of course if one believes that the power of God comes and goes, leaving him when he has had some signs of it, he will experience accordingly. Tell your healing power how its strength and quickness abide with you, increasing daily, your talks to the hidden energies of your being are either putting soldiers around them who will guard them from appearing outside, or they are setting the guards at naught.

What is your habit of speaking to your healing power? How do you speak of it? Some have put four quaternions of soldiers to guarding their healing powers and it is only by several nights spent in unceasing description of the healing Spirit that it comes forth freely to heal one case. The complainings and mournings and wonderings and lamentings because the healing power does not work through them quickly are quaternions of soldiers and stone prison walls to the healing energy.

How do you speak of your power of loving? How do you think of it? That loving power God gave you is eternal in its ministry. It need not be killed with the sword of persecution as James was by Herod. Do you think your love will cease because it is scorned? Do you think it is too weak to endure the desertion of those unto whom you sent its ministry? Tell the bright stream of your power of living, that it is warm and strong enough to melt all the hate of a world. Tell it nothing can withstand it. Tell it how wise it is in dealing with all people. It speaks a word here and keeps silent there. It defends a child here and supports a whole family there. Each energy has all the potency of all the ministry in its nature. Each energy is strong in wisdom, quick in healing, wise in speaking, able in supporting and defending.

Is it your habit to tell the twelve energies with which you are endowed how perfect they are? If not, spend as long time as this church did telling of Peter's free goodness. Then a maiden will report to you that Peter is come out of prison. That is, some credulous person will believe you have great healing power, great wisdom, strong powers of some kind, as Rhoda, the maiden, first heard the voice of the liberated Peter.

You will not believe that credulous character. You would rather a bank president or a city mayor told you that you had such liberated powers. Then if you do not really feel satisfied that there is Omnipotence in your healing power so that it can melt down every obstacle from your path, why you may hide it under another set of ideas, as they did Peter for new fear of Herod.

But the mighty doctrine still remains that the angel of the Lord forever encamppeth, the power of the Spirit is able for all things, and they shall not hurt or kill the Spirit set free at our will. Peter will continue knocking. Wisdom knocks without ceasing for approval. So we will without ceasing tell of its strength and quickness. We will exercise it on every little event of our life and on every stupendous occasion. Shall the insect under the buttercup have less attention to the paintings of its little back than Orion's belt in its splendor? Shall the minutest bit of good I would have brought to me have less of the strength of my wisdom or love than my destiny in the sum total of my life's happiness? As my purpose is utter consecration to untrammeled Truth, so is my purpose to make the daily lot of the newsboy and my boy one and the same in strength of beauty, freedom of wisdom, power in making the imprisoning notions of past teachings nothing — nothing at all.

What these two ranks of seekers go forth to seek they will find. It is not their good to win popular favor by shutting their wisdom and spiritual energies into the hidden places where they have been taught they are now kept only to be won forth by the terrible battle with ignorance. They shall hear the noble doctrine of Jesus that there is no danger in the pathway of Spirit, no failure in the judgment of the Divinity pressing for utterance at the gateway of every pore of their being.

The black man on the Saharan oasis shall not be sought for his rescue from evil. God shall be sought in his face and in his life. For what we go forth to find we shall find and how we proceed is according to what it is we proclaim we are seeking. What we do is the energy we liberate. We liberate what we choose. We are transcendent beings, using or not using our energies according as we choose.

The prison and cross is for them that seek them. The glory of Jesus in quick demonstration is for them that seek Him in all events. Ignorance and sin if you seek them; the goodness of God if you please. "Seek and ye shall find."

November 6, 1892

LESSON VIII

THE MINISTRY OF THE HOLY MOTHER

Acts 13:1-13

The people have always used two ways of bringing to pass life, health, strength, support, defense. Either by material performances or by spiritual exercises, great miracles and mighty improvements have resulted or failed to result. When life was to be saved, in great multitudes soldiers with sabers and guns have slain other multitudes to save it. If starvation stared a city in the face, its strong men tore down and pillaged other cities to get bread for that city, or cultivated patiently the seeds and soils to bring enough to the families. This is materiality, and its processes, sometimes peaceful, sometimes violent.

By spiritual or metaphysical processes, the same results have been reached without any such exertions of muscles or patient delvings as the material or physical ways demanded. Instances by the million are reported through the ages, how, by a metaphysical operation called prayer, miraculous things have been brought to pass. Elisha, a gentle prophet of Israel, a thousand years before Christ, came to the rescue of a besieged city, and by praying, caused a great abundance of provisions to be suddenly spread before the host of starving people. The king with his strong and willing army had utterly failed to bring the needed assistance.

Elisha could do great things and small things by the exercise of a metaphysical process called prayer. Nothing was too small and insignificant for him to pay loving and majestic attention to, and nothing was too great for the mighty sweep of his spiritually enlightened faculties. He was very like the Supreme Spirit, whose cooperation his prayers invoked, in the respectful tenderness with which he touched the tiny wants of little homes and the immense wants of kings and kingdoms.

The Supreme Spirit lights the flaming points of distant Arctos with glory and reddens the wings of the insect under the grasses. The great God delights to wheel in heavenly splendor the sunlit worlds of Canis Major at the foot of Orion, and to move in speechless happiness the microscopic infusoria swimming in speed around each other in the tumbler on your table. So Elisha raised up with tender kindness the Shunammitish baby, and drew the ax head from the bottom of the Jordan for the simple hearted laborers, exactly as readily as he opened the dropping globules of ether to disclose the heavenly hosts that loved him.

Hezekiah, after him, a king in whom the knowledge of the ways of that metaphysical Presence men have called God, was quickened, lifted up his voice and spake words whose import unlocked the gates of assistance where no material or physical power was available, and swept the fields of a host determined against him. Not a sign of harm was visible when the spiritual exercise of Hezekiah had wrought its mission.

"The King is not saved by the multitude of an host, neither the strong man by his valor" (Psalms 33:16), according to the spiritual doctrine of processes for demonstrating life, health, strength, support, defense. No gathering multitudes, no mechanics of civilization or barbarism, can match the sweep of a prayer, which has let loose the flood-gates of energy stored in the circumambient ethers around the heads of nations.

The company of Scotch Covenanters, whose enemies chased close — stopped at the sound of the voice of prayer of Saunders. "Spread thy cloak over us puir things," rose his childlike petition, and messengers of mercy dropped their soft robes down close, till like a fog of hiding the pitiful band were covered and the discomfited enemy turned back defeated. They call it a fog, but it was the hem of the mantle of protection whose white kindness touches the pillow where your head rests, ready any moment to be stronger than sorrow, more terrible than any army with banners, if you will but touch its sweet chords with the words of your heart.

Nothing material can reach it, nothing unjust or angry can stir it, though it is as willing as the mother who bent over your cradle, and as capable as your highest hopes could ask.

Choose, people, resting, walking, studying, competing, whether it is better worth while to get one with the Spirit brooding ever over and near and through all the earth, or to go on in the ways of the flesh whose competitions and strivings wear the heart sore and strike the hopes back till the skin is withered and the eyes have lost their light.

Ever anon the lovers of the spiritual ways have spoken, but the noise of the world has been too great for the sound of their teachings to touch that inner ear which must respond before the mind is willing to cease using the hands and brain of physical existence to bring to pass its assistance, its life, health, strength, support and defense. The noise of the world has even drowned the sound of their teachings to their own ears of those who have struggled to free themselves from the harrowing ways of materiality to be united with the peaceful successes of Spirit.

Ages ago, the Zoroastrian prophets taught a lesson of how to live by the Spirit out of the reach of the fret and turmoil of matter. Taking the wings of the words of faith, we rise into the airs out of the reach of pain, away from the lashings of fate, free from disappointments of trying to win our way in a world gathered to defeat our every purpose, they said. But a sound of the world's beliefs rose high on their bewildered ears, and they stopped to parley about what evil things the Spirit saw in different kinds of foods and the marriage of castes. So they drew the gates against the Spirit with as strong bars against its beautiful ministry as if they had been stone walls clinched with steel bolts. For the Spirit is only wooed by praises. She only moves down on the hosts embattled against us when we unlock the filmy gates between us by the keys the Truth in our hearts tells. The Spirit cannot look upon evil. She sees none in her life. She touches none in her pathway. When talk of evil begins, when scoldings or descriptions of troubles or wickedness begin, a gateway is closed against the glory-shod feet of the Holy Mother of mercy and love.

The Brahmins spoke of her white robes of healing and she let them fall over the bruised spots of their lives, ages and ages ago. Then they refused that those born in lowliness and those born as women should feel the touch of her seamless robe of healing, and closed the invisible gates against her streaming balsams of cure for all evils. For God, the maker of worlds, God the Father, is careful of God the Spirit, the Holy Spirit, the Mother, that she shall only go down where the gates of hiding are opened by truth. Praise without blame, kind words without tincture of censure, the Holy-

Motherhood of God may slip down through, and with the soft fingers of divine tenderness, smooth the brow of anguish or give the help you are needing.

The ministry of God is the Spirit of God, the Mother. The Mother is fair and kind and untouched by the name of sin, sickness or death. He who would live must open the gates for the Mother of Life by thoughts that eschew death. So Paul closed the gates against the Mother Spirit, the bride of God, the Father, and down falls the sight of poor Elymas (Acts 13:8-12). Tender words, gentle words of healing life, balming, lenitive, forgiving words would have opened the gates for the bride to walk through, that the perfume of her holiness might have seized the heart of Elymas to speak forth in raptures of the power of the Spirit of God as greater than all the acts of his legerdemain. He might have seen how sweetly mysterious, how strongly miraculous God as a Spirit can be, ministering unto the Sons and daughters who constitute the sonship of God in their divine nature. But Paul caught a sight of the blackness of sorcery and called Elymas such names as the ears of the Mother are never permitted to hear. The protecting Father hath a law that the mother ministry of the Spirit shall never pass through the walls where hard words are spoken.

"Make smooth the grasses,
Cover the pathway with leaves,
My bride's feet are sandaled for peace."

The early Church forgot this law of God the Father concerning the ministry of God, the Spirit Mother, and closed against her mercies, her kindness, again and again, till the healing of her seamless dress touching the bedsides of pain and disease was by and by lost sight of, and miracles have been so few that men have even doubted if the Spirit ever wrought any. There have been twelve messages, which the metaphysicians of the ages have given, which have had the opening of the closed gates in their strength and wisdom. The Spirit has stepped forth through them. John the Revelator called them foundation stones to the beautiful temple. He called them gates of pearl. Paul had been right in saying that we are the gates of God. He had spoken some of the messages with the unlocking skill in their meanings. The Spirit of God has always stepped into sight with the miracles of healing and uplifting and comforting wherever they have been spoken. All the world which has had freedom from speaking the words the Healing Mother must not hear, have agreed in the messages or statements which make straight and smooth her pathway over the needs of mankind. We now call them the twelve doctrines of Jesus; the twelve messages of Christ; the twelve lessons of Science.

The early wise men called them the twelve genii of power; the twelve powers of strength; the twelve energies of being. Here at the center we dwell. There at the gates dwelleth she. It is ours to open the gates. It is hers to enter in through the gates. "Go through — go through all the gates to make way for the people," cried the prophet. Letting Paul's closing down of the Spirit aside, seeing the opening of the gates of the loving deputy's mind, we will mention the true ways of Jesus. We will touch the hinges of pearl that from this moment we may not hide the ministry of the motherhood of God.

Did you ever notice how careful the noblest and tenderest husbands are that their beautiful wives shall hear nothing hard or pain giving? They are the living symbols of the carefulness of God the Father that the Spirit, the Holy Spirit, shall not be found where censure, criticism, scolding, maligning, crying are going on. The filmy walls between her merciful ears and our harshness are as thick as the stones of the ancient prison walls so far as her hearing is concerned. Yet she is near, close, ready, all-powerful, all-capable, empowered with the signet ring of God, the Omnipotent Father, to hear all our prayers. Open the gateway to her ministry of a new life by telling what her blessed ears may hear about life.

So she will stream into your soul with a new life quickening and forth from your soul will go to the dying a stream of that ministry called raising the dead, which Jesus, whose ever-present Mother she was, brought to pass so often. We may let her in by telling things to her about health, which the

Protecting Father would willingly let her listening ears hear.

Do you know the second message of Science concerning health? It is the only one, which she may enter into your soul by and go forth where your heart chooses to heal and cure the hurts of the world.

There is a third message. It is about strength. If you are ready to speak as the Father permits the spiritual strength to hear, she will revive your energies, and up will spring the strength of those where you would have strength transform out of weakness.

The fourth is what she is ready to do about supporting you without your struggling against any odds. The Spirit would have you as satisfied as she is with home, bread, and wine, and milk, and honey. But she may only hear the fourth message of Science concerning support. You may rest back of the gateway of plenty till you give her the open sesame the Father will let her come in by.

She will shelter you and the world if you will let her in by the fifth message of Science. She may go before like a wing of defense where the danger is lurking, and no ill shall befall where you speak the safe words for her to hear concerning defense.

The sixth will give you the character presence, which high thoughts on majestic themes can give. She will show you how to think so as to be the

Gardieus stone, shining as one whose soul converses with the immortals.

The seventh she has consecrated to the spoken word. She will speak with a voice, and speak through your voice so that the ears of the people will sharpen and their hearts shall leap at your words. The sound of your voice may be full of healing, full of uplifting. She will touch your pen with the fire of inspiration if you are bold enough to tell her those words about writing things of great purport, which the Father gives her permission to hear. She will touch your throat with songs of the cherubim and seraphim, chanting great symphonies around the seas at the foot of the mountains of paradise, if you will tell her what God is giving her ears to hear, about the voice that enchants with melodies that cause the hills to drop down their odors of healing and apples of bliss. She can make your fingers supple and skillful if you know the words about skill, when she, bending low by your pillow, may hear.

She can make you so beautiful that the beggars will forget to be hungry. Her smile may light on your face with its own Love-lit glory, if you know the eleventh message the great God calls the opening of the gateway to the sight of her face.

She will teach you how to love so that all hate shall be melted where you speak and where your face is seen. The genius for loving so that anger is smiled into peace, the genius for loving so that sorrow shall rest into gladness, she can enter into your soul with and pass over the world with.

You must make her hear by the twelfth message of Science, which is the only one the great love of God permits her to hear.

She was bending close over Paul, but he would not open the door by the key, which his heart held in a secret recess. If he had given the Holy Mother the twelfth message of Science, Elymas would not have been struck blind. No, he would have loved Paul with the love of a brother, and gone with him over the cities where he knew their secrets, showing him all things in patience and sweetness. The Scriptures are given for warnings. This lesson is a warning. Do not think the mother tenderness of the omnipotent God as spirit of miracle-working ever hurts. It is when words are spoken her ears are protected from hearing, that blindness and pain and disappointment fall to the lot of the world. God is good. The Spirit is love. The miracles of Spirit are for joyous fulfillment of hopes. Whisper the words to the ears of the Mother. Let down the bars between her ever Presence and thee. She will enter in and go forth clad with the miracles of Jesus.

Let him that heareth come! Let him that is athirst come! None is so lowly, none is so wicked, but she will bend and hear, if he will not use the words the Father never permits her to hear. She is wooed by praises; she hears great praises of God the Father. She loves the descriptions of His majesty, His mercy, His watch-care, His omnipotent love. Do you know the words the Father openeth the ears of the Spirit to hear?

Addendum: The Twelve Gates can be found in Series Three, January 10, 1892.

November 13, 1892

LESSON IX

POWER OF LOFTY IDEAS

Acts 13:26-43

If a person is in great trouble and affliction, he should make the highest and most Spiritual affirmation that has ever struck his mind as a beautiful truth of God. He should keep on repeating that idea in his mind till affliction is left behind. He will then be delighted to find that he is stronger, more buoyant, wiser than he ever was in his life before. The trouble has not left him the worse for wear, because it has not touched him. His lofty idea only has touched him. Keep it as a rule of mind in the time of great persecution by circumstances or people, no matter how they come to pass with you. Touch not the earth; touch God. Here Paul tells of how, by the high arm of God, the Israelites were brought out of Egypt. They took their highest ideals of Spiritual power and held to them while they were in sore distress. Our highest ideals are the strong arm of God leading out of whatever bondage we seem to be in.

Paul immediately goes on to say that God destroyed seven nations in the land of Canaan. God never destroys anything. If, while we are looking straight into this Spiritual Presence, full of goodness and peace, we keep speaking of God's making men so constituted that they cheat, hate, fight, then those words come back upon us in a crowd of people who misuse us. We do not need to say God ordained it or made our life lines to run in misery. We must be free from our ideas if we would run on smooth life lines. Some of the finest minds through the ages have discovered the marked and immediate connection between ideas and events; they have left out one proposition which now we use — change ideas and events change; drop ideas and events cease.

Paul here says that God suffered their manners forty years in the wilderness. God suffers nothing. He endures nothing. The Israelites in the wilderness simply spoke halfway and compromising texts concerning delivery from bondage, therefore they took extra time to get out of desponding conditions. Hope and faith must unite in the mind to bring strong, quick deliverance from your hardships.

Notice that children have just as much faith that miracles of help will be wrought as the parents' hope will let them have. A child's confidence runs up to the express expectation or hope of the mother. "God will hear us when we have scraped the bottom of the meal barrel, Mamma." "I hope so." If the mother had taught the child that there is no such thing as the bottom to a meal barrel, his confidence would have run up to that teaching. That family would always be provided with abundance of meal. Let the mother's teaching run buoyantly and hopefully up to the idea that there is nothing on the earth but what they can have in full, rich, bountiful abundance, and up the child's confidence will run to meet and mingle with the teaching till the earth with her bounty comes hurrying to fulfill the faith of the child.

Has God changed toward the mother and the child? Did God suffer because the meal barrel was empty, or rejoice because it was full?

Does the mathematical principle you are dealing with suffer when you say you have got your problem all wrong because you said if X squared is 64, then X must be 7. No, X will always equal 8, if its square is 64, no matter what you say. You need not lay your misery to the Principle we know as God if you will tell how God made your happiness less or more. You shall lay your misery to your ideas of God, not to God.

Paul often rose to stupendous metaphysics, as when he said, "We can do nothing against the Truth, but only for the Truth." The Truth shines the clearer to us when we see how unalterable and how uncajoleable it is. If the Israelites complain about Truth because it did not hurry them out of trouble, they never touched Truth, which is supremely free from trouble. If nations fell back when they appeared, then nations fell back because they had confidence in the hopes of their leaders. They believed as high as their teachers taught them they might. They were free as far as they heard and had confidence in Truth. If a doctor goes into the sick room and tells his patient with buoyant cheerfulness that he is sure to get well, the patient will get well if the doctor's hope strikes the faith cord of the patient. If the doctor has such buoyant cheer right straight along and never lets his mind get nipped by that hidden fear of evil which his mind keeps in his cellar, the patient's faith will get hot enough to take him into splendid health. Thus two of them together work the cure right through the sickness. Hope and Truth and faith in Truth are quick freedom from evil.

The whole of faith and the whole of hope ought to be united in every mind. The Jews of old had covenanted with God for a Messiah to come in the process of time. They also covenanted that the Jews should refuse him when he did come. So it all came to pass. But the everlasting Truth still remained that the Messiah was then with them and able to save them from trouble and hunger any moment.

Paul refers to the time when the Jews had been so self-willed that they would have a personal king. He then shows how David, the shepherd boy, came up as a fruit of their strong will, which sometimes drooped into sweet meekness. If this strong will is in one mind, it will drive its life environment all askew. If you have a strong will, you must be exceedingly meek to listen to the word of those people who get on in the world by high principles. The strong will bending to hear a great principle suddenly strikes fire, and the clear and beautiful judgment rises. Martin Luther was not nearly so brilliant and able by scholarship or native talent as Melanchthon, but he was more meek to his religious teachers, consequently there came a moment when his judgment stood upright on its feet. He had come to the fruiting time of will crossing with docility. There is great strength always born with good judgment. He was strong to proclaim his new confidence that it is not by works that we get spiritual but by faith.

The commonest intellect, with the poorest sort of education, will be enabled by the union of will and meekness to sit in council halls as wise and sound in judgment. Without docility such a character is obstinate and stupid. Always there is one idea to gather ourselves to and rise within — on the union of it with our strongest trait — into freedom, peace, wisdom. The genius along any line should speak out and think out the science of the art he is the master of. Gasner, the matchless healer, could not explain, on scientific principles, the process by which he healed the multitudes. Consequently the science of his healing was as invisible after his brilliant cures as before he touched Germany with the comfort of his presence.

It is exactly as if the mathematical genius should be able to tell mankind about the coming conjunctions and transits of heavenly bodies by lightning-like calculations from first principles, but could not explain how he did it to his admiring fellowmen.

Every brilliant cure has its perfect explanation. He who shall arise with a good explanation of how he brings to pass instantaneous bodily cures will be the Jesus Christ of the age unto which he comes. His own body must be perfect. It must vibrate to the touch of his Science as blissfully as Paganini's violin lifted and enchanted his audience when his fingers of fire from immortal altars quickened its fibres.

It is by the twelve lessons in law and twelve lessons in gospel, united in one mind, that success is best manifest. One by one the conditions of our human lot are transformed as we go on from mountain top to mountain top of thought about God. We learn that we do not need to tie to even the loftiest Truth we have so far realized. The Jews did not need to fulfill the prophesies of their fathers. They did not need to pin to a tradition that they should hang on a tree the Lord of all the earth when He came. We do not need to pin ourselves to the doctrine that the just shall live by faith if we have found that life is forever in us, whether we believe it or not.

Martin Luther held himself pinned to the fourth mountain top of Science till he wrought out the freedom of a planet from the idea of living by works. But when the gentle Zwingli offered him the hand of love and friendship, independent of doctrinal differences, he had the offer of his lifetime to spring to the heights of a principle more glorified than his mind had touched, namely, "He who loves me transcends me." Doctrine to the winds when friendship lights the hilltops! Was not true friendship, love in the heart, able to cause difference of opinion to be nothing?

It would not have hurt his doctrine, but would have untied him from a post to which he was gathering himself if he had accepted the loving friendship of Zwingli. He who ties to an idea is as struck with death as he who ties to a tree in the wilderness.

There is always something dead in the body of him who tries to tie others to his ideas, for the chain around the ankle of the slave is clasped around the neck of the captor. If you do not believe in tobacco, that is no reason why your mind should tie your neighbor to your idea of tobacco. Mentally take your clutch off him, and, being free from the chain of your censure, he will rise up to a clearer sight of what it is his soul seeks. He will be more healthy. You will suddenly be free from a burden of your life. You have been tied to your own opinions and have tried to tie others to them. From the time you take the yoke of your opinions off your sons and your neighbors' sons, so dead sure you are right and they wrong, they will breathe the air of goodness and you will rise free from that physical disease or pain that represents death through being tied to ideas.

Paul agrees in this, Acts 13, like a person in a nightmare, with the idea that the prophesies of evil must be fulfilled. He agrees like a person half-waking with the promise, "God shall raise him from the dead". This is true. This moment dead hopes will arise if you let go your ideas of what people ought not to do and what they have done that you do not think is right. In all the universe, there is only yourself and God to describe. Yourself, as rejoicing in the peace and love of God, and God as all that is good. Paul should rise to the Absolute of the promises. He should get clear from traditions. No corruption for any man more than for Christ, for God is freedom. No death when we speak truths, for God is freedom from death. No burdens, for God is freedom. No pain, for God is freedom. No prophesies, for God is freedom from prophesies. No waiting, for God is NOW freedom. Mind is free to be as wise, as great, as powerful, as it has courage to let go its past ideas. God has no ideas of the past. God is freedom of ideas, past or future. Therefore unhitched from opinions, we are free as God. Paul refused his freedom. We receive ours.

November 20, 1892

LESSON X

SURE RECIPE FOR OLD AGE

Acts 13:44-52 Acts 14:1-7

There is in the spiritual pharmacopia a sure recipe for old age. You will remember that Thoreau speaks of the young man as a demigod, because his thoughts are only half in sympathy with the earth; the other half is still clinging to the glory that he had with the Father before the world was. It is by letting go his hold on the expectation that Divinity will prevail and the hosts of God will miraculously interpose in his behalf that he gets way-wised to earth and uses the world's methods with greater or lesser success. Then, instead of stepping from the prime of manhood into the glorious beauty and power ordained for him from the foundations of being, he gets watery eyeballs, brittling limbs, grisly cuticle. This is called old age. But no man would ever have stepped from the aspirations of youth with its way-winning beauty into the estate of old age if he had chosen at the flood tide of opportunity to let go the world's ideas rather than to let go expecting the Spirit of Glory to do all things.

The little child's thoughts do always behold the face of pure goodness. Youth and early manhood have not yielded quite their ears and eyes to the voices and sights telling things of evil. And if only the things of Spirit should ever be told them there would never be any sign of decrepitude and mortality's mold creeping over them. Who told the child that danger lurked in his pathway? Did you? Was not the Spirit within him strong with the safety of the Spirit without him, stronger than all the dangers you could imagine, till he listened to you and let go his own inheritance of safety eternal? Is it not Satan tempting the innocent over again every time we prognosticate hurt? Would it not be more like taking a draught from the walls of the Spirit of youth for us to see as the child sees, speak as he speaks, expect as he expects, than to be his so-called wise guardians, careful instructors, grave forewarners of evil?

To the church this mighty doctrine of eternal youth was intrusted. She has struck the rim of her own old age by describing the pitfalls that lie in the pathway of youth, and the mold of the lack of honest confidence in her goodness has begun to wizen her pulpits. So to the Gentiles, those who could not believe that if God is good and occupies all space and all place He could call a Son to die, or a world into hardship, is now given the doctrine of Jesus, that whoever tells Truth does not fail or die he becomes transfigured in the sight of the nations. At the floodtide of his letting go of the religions that urge him to beware of evil he finds himself absolved from the world, free as the Elohim on the joyous streets of the city of God.

Transfiguration is the birthright of man. *"Where I am there ye may be also."* He who rejects everything except the real meanings of the teachings of Jesus ascends into His glory. "Understanding is a well-spring of Life." As the body thrives in appearance by assimilating right food, so the mind quickens and gleams by eating of the doctrine as Jesus did truly give it to man. Every time the mind understands a principle of good, it increases in stature. If you see that it is perfectly safe to tell children their nature is God and their pathway is absolute safety. That seeing is a new quickening of your mind. If you do not see it your mind must have some other idea ministered unto it. If you see that it is as if you had loaded yourself with barrels of stones to have listened to ideas of defeat, disaster, injustice, as part of the intention of God for your life to meet, when that was never the plan of the Divine Goodness with you, you will breathe freely and rise with new buoyancy upon agreement with Truth.

In this thirteenth chapter of Acts, from the forty-fourth verse, we see the process of perfect doctrine as it has risen for the religions of the world to accept. They turn from its light, but the so-called irreligious, or Gentiles, receive it gladly.

This lesson is an object lesson. We are the people meant. If we have understanding that all is mind, not materiality nor persons, we will see that the light that shines now among us is the speech of unresisted Truth. Whoever lets Truth be expressed in unresisted freedom through him rises as on wings out of the reach of his daily encounters with the world. There is nothing he fears. Sickness drops off. Misfortune glides out of his reach. Fears that his children or good name will fail do not come nigh him. As he thus gets freer and freer he is not aware of himself as a "demi-god", but God.

The glory of the church of the Jews was that by the preaching of the Presence of God, that Presence came visibly into their midst. The receptivity of the Gentiles was the spread of the manifest God. As it is written, "Light to lighten the Gentiles and the glory of my people Israel."

So it is today. It is the glory of the church that she has preached the goodness of God and the second coming of His Presence, till now the idea of His goodness permits no mixture of accusation against Him as laying schemes in our pathway to test our quality, nor slaying a son to evidence His loving kindness; till now we understand the second coming to be the unresisted proclamation of the absolute Good.

The power of the Holy Ghost is on them and in them that let it be known that the life-inspiring Spirit is now moving in unthreatened splendor from mind to mind over the earth. The healing

Spirit is running with unassailable purity from life to life the round planet over. The strengthening Spirit goes forth with irresistible vigor from heart to heart. The sustaining and supporting Spirit blows aside the mantle of poverty and despair, and those with their hands on the products of nature cannot hold even a loaf from a child, so overpowering is the breath of the Name of Him who stands now in the earth. The defending Spirit tenderly smoothes out the pathway of man so that today there can be no ill come nigh the dwelling of him who knows that he was never meant to believe the teachings of a God who needed propitiating. He whose face is set to the doctrine now come sees that every hurt, every accident, every disaster, has come from the doctrine of propitiation for sins. Whoever lets fall that idea is free to walk boldly through these days which have come as the fruition of that age-old idea of a Creator who needed to be bought off from His anger. Strikes and embezzlements and hospitals full of groanings all stand forth as the fruitage of holding the youth of the world to such teachings concerning the dealings of the God of Heaven with man, as drag them in mind to think that a friend of the Divinity woos in their bosoms. So the weary old age of the earth now lies down defeated. "The earth waxes old as a garment."

But the mind that is God is set free to think through all who do not play the part of the Jews in this lesson. They shine and glow and invigorate with a life not of the earth. A new mind rises, a new mind sends over the world thoughts that take them that think into the mountains of safety. The speaking forth of the Mind of God is the trumpet that sounds in these days as Paul and Barnabas sounded in their day. At the sound of the word of Truth, a whole disease melts away into the mists of nowhere. At the sound of a spoken word the diseased earth shall melt with fervent heat and the skies roll away like a scroll. They are all, as they stand out, formulated of the teachings given to the children concerning the Maker of heaven and earth.

The recording Spirit is given unresisted freedom to write on the stones and in the sands that that which is true must reign now from henceforth; not what is false. The joyous Spirit sings of what has already come to pass, now that the doctrine of Jesus is preached. The skill-inspiring Spirit is not hindered as it touches the fingers of youth with eternal genius of an order needing no schools or ships or apprenticeship to teach how to handle the white Substance that waits in the airs for the fingers that are moved by the Mind of God to make those new clothes and new houses to live in, foretold by the prophets for this age to fulfill. The judgment and beauty of Truth are set free. There is none to resist the beauty of judgment and the judgment of beauty, which is Jesus Christ named in the mind. The love-inspiring Spirit is moving with unresisted freedom, declaring that to them that see her lifting the veil of the false thought of ages there is now liberty and delight, with no bondage to hurt or fear.

Here it tells how the multitude of the city was divided, part holding with the Jews and part holding with the Apostles. Now, they who still hold to the doctrine of worthiness, shedding of blood for sins, the cross, the necessity for evil, may turn over into the worldly signals of senility, while they who hear the Spiritual winds sifting through the noisy sounds of materiality may go from city to city preaching the immortal beauty that wakes to never glory in him who keeps hold of his birthright.

November 27, 1892

LESSON XI

THE HEALING PRINCIPLE

Acts 14:8-22

In the year 1814 a young Japanese by the name of Kurozumi Sakyo lay in what his doctors pronounced to be the last stages of consumption. It was his pious daily custom to worship the sun and his ancestors, also the celestial and terrestial kami. One day he resolved that when, after his death, he himself should become a kami (deified spirit) he would devote all his time to healing the diseases of mankind. His devotions were always marked by a peculiar gratefulness of feeling towards the sun and the kami of his parents. He did not beg for favors like most devotees. His prayers were not petitions; they were loving thanksgivings.

One day it occurred to him that he ought to bless and give thanks to heaven for every tiniest event and object. As everything he possessed, great or small, had come from above, it must all in turn be remembered in his loving thanksgivings.

By thus resolving upon a still further exercise of his mind and feelings he began to experience a new cheerfulness. Certain Japanese believe that continual cheerfulness invokes a positive spirit, Yoki. They believe that all disease has its rise in someone's yielding to the spirit of gloom, Inki.

Kurozumi did not look to be healed of consumption. He had not asked to be healed; but while he was at the very ebb-tide of his malady, with his heart entirely absorbed in thanking the sun for its marvelous goodness in giving him so many friends and such a good home, he rose suddenly, strong and renewed. He was in perfect health. A miracle had been wrought. He began to be so ecstatically grateful to his god that a still further miracle was wrought upon him. He breathed in the positive Yoki or cheerful spirit so intensely that his breath became vivified. He found that it would heal every sort and kind of disease and soothe the sharpest pains. He thus began while yet in life to breathe upon sick and diseased mankind that healing principle he had supposed he must wait till after death to exercise.

From that time on his grateful patients and their families regarded him as a living Kami. He had spent three years in honest expressions of gratitude for what other people considered only the commonest procession of favors from heaven, when the cheerful spirit, Yoki, took absolute control of his life, even unto the healing power. It became an elixir vital, a renewal of vitality, to his wasted body.

We see by this true event that the descriptions of the goodness of deity which the very devoted have ever given us are those which have in their nature a potency that will operate if they are continued as mental exercises, prompted by the will to do right for its own sake. If the young Japanese had been three years practicing giving thanks as a species of Spiritual gymnastics whereby he hoped to attain health, he might not have felt very grateful even then, while his racking cough and feeble limbs reminded him that there was something he did not feel just right about. He looked into the face of the spirit of the sun and told it of its own goodness without any purpose of any sort in his heart. Yet health came as a natural outcome of the daily elation of all his thoughts by the words he had spoken. His words generated a warm feeling. The feeling and words generated an elixir which formulated a healthy body.

There is something in the being of deity which calls for our delight in it, whether it is filling every vacant spot in our sphere of life or not. We can look beyond our ideas of our own lot in life, and away from all that we have experienced, into the great fact of a good beyond good, and there will be a nameless pleasure in this sight that will open our lips to speak praises we cannot help feeling.

Often people who are greatly irritated by their environments can look beyond their feelings and thoughts into the great fact of their being something too great and too calm to be like their affairs, and that sight, if only for one second's space, is a rest of soul for which they are grateful. To prolong the sight is to feel the elevation of soul that is its still further rest. And still deeper pleasure compels newer words of thanksgiving. Some do go through all the items of their human possessions with honest praise of their Giver, up into sudden moments of facing that great fact of being, and down from that sight of the Presence which is not moved by the excitements of pleasures or pains they come buoyant and transformed.

This going by the pathway of praises was the method of Kurozumi.

Looking beyond all things and beyond all ideas, into the nameless Presence, beyond the God described by mankind, Mary, the Mother of Jesus, watched the stirless Being of true Deity, and that immaculate sight brought forth a Messiah. All the highest words of her most devout descriptions of God now formulated into her sight.

Doctrine of Jesus is a way of bringing to pass all the affairs and events of life by a way that is easy, a burden that is light. It is this doctrine of looking away from the ideas we think and the emotions we feel into this Presence which has never been described in words, but which, when Kurozumi stepped into sight of it, brought forth his healing, and which, when Mary saw by that inner sight we are all capable of exercising, brought forth the long-expected Messiah, "Rest in the Lord and He shall bring it to pass." Kurozumi passed into speechless and thoughtless ecstacy by words of brightness. We need not go by words or thoughts into sight of this changeless, moveless Principle we call God; we may recognize its vicinity and wait for effects. Its effects are the sweetest fulfillments of mighty miracles.

"I will make a new covenant with you." "Cast all your care on God, for He careth for you." Under this direction let now your covenant with the omnipotent Spirit be that you will do nothing either to benefit or prolong your life; the Mighty God, ever present, shall care entirely for your life. You will not do anything either to benefit or perfect your health or strength; the Mighty God, waiting in eternal majesty near you, shall do all that needs doing for your health and your strength. Neither for support nor defence will you lift your efforts, the sustaining and upholding Spirit of good shall support and defend your life.

The deep thought and quickening speech of Omnipotence shall do your thinking and speaking. The words that you write and the praises you sing shall come from your sight of the ever-abiding Principle that asks nothing of you, but covenants with you to do all works for you, whose immaculate sight, unsmirched by intentions to struggle and strive, has caught the elixir which falls into the soul of him whose faith rests for the Lord to bring to pass.

The genius for action is born of a speechless sight of the actionless Being of God, as Jesus was born of Mary's speechless conception of the Presence of God. Covenant with the Presence Unnamable, the everlasting Spirit we speak of as God, for your beauty. Let it inspire you with the genius for loving and being loved, as Mary let it inspire her with the genius for bringing forth the only Lover the world ever knew.

Look into this fourteenth chapter of Acts, and find the verses where Paul, who had praised Jesus Christ till the electric fires of the mighty Name had made his eyes and voice alive -with the healing principle, faced the Spirit, and waited to bring forth the cure of the cripple of Lystra. After "steadfastly beholding", his voice commanded with power. Then, exactly as the people tried to make out that Kurozumi was a superior being come among them, so did the Gentiles offer to worship Paul and Barnabas. But Kurozumi, of Japan, with his praise of the sun stepping into ecstatic vision of God; Paul and Barnabas stepping by praises of Jesus into glorified sight of the Presence of Spirit; many walking in maidenly whiteness over the silver stones of beautiful prayers — none of these was a being superior to those they walked among. *"I said ye are gods." "Ye are all sons of the Most High."* Ye are beings, all, of transcendent powers. The grandeur of supernal Presence enshrouds you all and waits for you to let go your clutch on the vanities of old ways of doing. The Gentiles who offered oxen and garlands, and would have done sacrifice unto Paul and Barnabas, were only ourselves, when we are offering our efforts and strivings, willing to sacrifice ourselves for the reformation and redemption of a world God finished in beauty and love and waits for us to see as He sees it.

The perfect creation waits ever near us. Looking into its changeless, moveless splendour Mary brought into our sight Jesus, one of the glorified inhabitants of the City of God. We, looking into this country, its stretches of fields elysian and hilltops of light we call air enswathing us, may catch a vision true enough to bring to the sight of our race other inhabitants of the golden-walled temples of heaven.

Here it tells that we shall enter this kingdom of heaven only by much tribulation (Verse 22). But this is because we believe in doing and clutching, and striving, and working to do our duty toward enlightening, redeeming, civilizing the world. Paul and Barnabas believed in struggling and striving to convert the people. It was as if many had struggled and striven to bring forth Jesus Christ. It took the silent sight of the abyss of Deity, deep of soul calling unto deep of soul, for Jesus, the inhabitant of the Heavenly City, to come stepping into the manger of Bethlehem. It takes the enraptured silence of our yielded life for the heavenly hosts of God to come walking down as on highways into the midst of this age.

But it is here. "Hark the herald angels sing." We do not try to improve or redeem the race; we stop here to see the race as God sees it. And over the highways of our immaculate silence troops of Elohim come nearer and nearer. Here in the workshop of the mystery of mind we find that secret of God which is the revealment of good. That which Mary did by making a pathway of effortless silence, over which walked our beloved King, we may do for all the inhabitants of descending Jerusalem. With one foot on the sea and one on the land, the angel proclaims that time shall be no more with the acceptance of this, the doctrine of Jesus. "He careth for you." On the swift thoughts which are the flowing seas, let the angel put one foot to indicate the subjection of thought. On the old doctrines in which we have settled beliefs, let the angel put one foot to proclaim that we surrender our creeds and our doctrines of salvation, redemption, reformation, of everything to the silence of the great, perfect world of God, which was in the beginning, is now, and ever shall be, "very good", as God sees it forever.

Kurozumi breathed the electric elixirs of a swift sight of the great fact of a nameless Presence here on earth. We will gather to the deeps of our being the elixirs of long, speechless knowledge that God is here. As He healed the sick, as Paul and Barnabas healed and called multitudes to hear their words, because of swift, speechless sights of God, so we, by abiding in the knowledge that healing comes from sight of God and not effort to find God or please Him, will hear the voices of the myriad hosts chanting great songs of gladness that we have made holy highways for them to walk over into our midst.

December 4, 1892

LESSON XII

WASHINGTON'S VISION

Acts 15:12-29

There is always something or someone near every one of us telling us the wisest course to pursue. If we learn to be observing and to have our minds made up to an issue, we shall have clear sight and hearing to receive right directions. The Oriental metaphysicians found out that to cease from thinking is a clarifying process for the mind; so they practiced ceasing from thoughts. They wondered greatly why the nameless satisfaction they were seeking did not result to them by the clarifying process of non-thinking. They never found out formerly, and have not yet been told, that if the mind is positively set upon any conviction it is locked in the prison of that conviction. Stopping thoughts only shuts the few port-holes and windows of the prison; it does not break down the walls of a mighty conviction. There was not an Eastern mystic who was not convinced clear to the roots of his mind that God ordained castes and sex inferiorities. Six thousand years of cessation of thought would not moulder the walls of that gloomy conviction.

The Occidental metaphysician now practices cessation from thinking because he has been told that it is wonderfully clarifying to the mind to stop thinking. He also is surprised to find how far away the glory of the satisfaction he hopes for still remains. He stopped thinking, while his mind was set as the everlasting hills into the determination to be recognized by his fellow beings as of some consequence, or as a mighty character. He hopes for the plaudit, "Well done". This also is a prison house with walls unmeltable by silence at the roots of mind.

When one is very sincere he is very opened. He may not be as able as his fellow men as regards talents or education, but he will have such open ears for the counsels that lie around him that his wisdom will be the marvel of his age.

George Washington was a genuine lover of his cause. The preservation of the independence of his country was to him his God-called mission. Recognizing the hand of the free God in the strike of America for liberty, he flung his life to the winds of the principle the strike represented.

The following narrative was related by Anthony Sherman, an octogenarian, who heard the account from Washington's own lips:

> "The darkest period of our Republic was the year 1777, when Washington, after experiencing

many reverses, went into winter quarters at Valley Forge. Often I observed tears course down the cheeks of our beloved Commander when he was considering the sufferings of his brave soldiers. Washington was in the habit of praying in secret and calling upon God for assistance, and it was only by the help of God we passed safely through those days of adversity.

One day Washington spent the whole afternoon in his room alone. When he came out I observed that he was much paler than usual, when he related to me the following:

"Whilst I was sitting at my table this afternoon engaged in writing and my mind heavy with sorrow, I suddenly observed directly opposite to me a most beautiful female.

I was so much surprised, for I had given strict orders not to be disturbed, that I could not find words at the moment to inquire the object of this unexpected visit. Two, three, and even four times I repeated the question without receiving an answer, the only effect being that she raised her eyes a little, I now experienced a most curious sensation spread over my whole body. I wished to rise from my seat, but the steady gaze of my mysterious visitor kept me spellbound. I again tried to speak to her, but my tongue was tied. An unknown, mysterious irresistible power had taken me prisoner. I could do nothing else but steadily gaze at the apparition. Gradually the room filled with light, and the form grew more clear and bright. My feelings were those of a dying man; I could neither think nor act. My steady gaze at the figure was all I was aware of.

I now heard a voice which said: 'Son of the Republic, behold and learn!' At the same time the figure stretched out its arm and pointed with its finger towards the east. Light clouds arose in the distance, which dispersed and revealed to my eyes a most astonishing picture. Before me all the countries of the earth were spread out, Europe, Asia, Africa, and America. Between Europe and America I saw the waves of the Atlantic Ocean toss backward and forward, and between America and Asia the waves of the Pacific Ocean.

Again I heard the voice: 'Son of the Republic, behold and learn!' Immediately a dark form like that of an angel appeared over the ocean between Europe and America. It then dipped water from the ocean with both hands, and with its right sprinkled it over America and with its left over Europe. Immediately dark clouds arose from both of these countries, which met in the middle of the ocean; here they remained stationery for awhile, then moved westward and wrapped America in darkness. Lightning flashed through the dark clouds, and I heard the groaning and shrieking of the American people. Again the angel dipped water from the ocean and sprinkled it as before. The black clouds withdrew and sank into the sea.

For the third time I heard the voice: 'Son of the Republic, behold and learn!' I looked towards America and saw populous villages and cities from the Atlantic Coast to the Pacific Ocean. Again I heard the mysterious voice: 'Son of the Republic, the end of the century is near at hand.

Behold and learn!' The dark form of the angel then turned toward the south, and coming from Africa, I observed a horrible phantom making its way to our country. It floated slowly and heavily over our towns and the country; the inhabitants arose to make war on each other and formed in battle array. As I looked at this scene I observed an angel surrounded with light; on his head he wore a beautiful crown on which was inscribed the word 'Union'. In his hand he held the American flag. This he planted between the contending armies, crying out: 'Remember you are brothers.' Immediately the nations threw away their arms, became friends again, and gathered around the flag.

Again I heard the mysterious voice: 'Son of the Republic, the second danger is past; behold and learn!' And I saw the villages and cities steadily increase in size and number until the whole country was covered with them — the whole extent, from the Atlantic to the Pacific, and the nation had multiplied in as countless numbers as the stars in heaven, or the sands on the seashore. Again I heard the voice: 'Son of the Republic, the end of the century is at hand; behold and learn!' The dark angel then put a trumpet to his mouth, blew it three times, then dipped out some water from the sea with his hand over Europe, Asia and Africa. My eyes now beheld a most terrible scene. From each of these countries dark heavy clouds arose and united in one mass; through this mass dark red lightning played. I saw troops of armed men advancing, and then sail across the sea to America, which was immediately covered by the black cloud.

And I saw how these immense armies desolated the land and laid towns and villages in ashes. I heard the roar of cannon, the clashing of swords, the cry of the victorious and vanquished millions engaged in deadly strife, when again I heard the mysterious voice proclaim: 'Son of the Republic, behold and learn!' The dark angel then again took up the trumpet and gave one long and terrible blow. Suddenly a light burst forth and drove away the dark cloud hovering over America. At the same time I saw the angel with the beautiful crown, on which was inscribed the word 'Union', descend from heaven, holding in one hand the star-spangled banner and in the other a sword, and accompanied by legions of heavenly spirits. These united with the American people when the latter were almost overpowered, who took fresh courage and formed in battle array. Again, amid the horrible noise of war, I heard the mysterious voice: 'Son of the Republic, behold and learn!'

After this voice the dark angel dipped out water for the last time from the sea and sprinkled it over America, and immediately the dark cloud retreated with its armies, which it had brought along, leaving the victory to the Americans.

I then again saw towns and villages rise in the same places where they had stood before, while the heavenly angel planted the star spangled banner among the people with a loud voice: 'As long as the stars are in heaven and as long as the dews descend from heaven to earth, so long shall this Republic exist.'

At the same time he took the beautiful crown from his head, on which was inscribed the word 'Union,' placed it on the star-spangled banner, and, kneeling down, cried out, 'Amen.' The apparition then began to dissolve, and at last the mysterious female was all that remained before me in my room, and again I heard the voice: 'Son of the Republic, what you have seen is explained as follows:

'Three dangers will come over this Republic. The second is most to be dreaded. When this one is past the whole world cannot conquer her. Let every child of the Republic learn to serve his God, his country and the Union.'

With these words the form vanished. I arose from my chair with the conviction that the birth, progress, and fate of the United States of America had been revealed to me."

These words, said Mr. Sherman, he heard from General Washington's own lips.

We know that the first two sections of the vision have been fulfilled. The last is now upon us. The reason for so vivid a picturing of the future of his country before him was because he needed a strong reassurance from some quarter. He had come to where he could not be pacified with the ordinary helps of his mind's reasonings or his religious convictions.

We, who are genuinely in earnest with respect to our lofty purposes, can be as plainly reassured of victorious freedom from whatever bondage we experience as the lover of the Republic was. Keep on knowing that you are a transcendent being with transcendent powers. This is honoring the handiwork of the Omnipotent Mind that sent you forth. It is a principle as worthy of espousing as the principle of liberty for a people whose property and labors are owned by a foreign nation.

The principle you espouse who take the Name of Jesus Christ as the synonym for Truth, Life, Freedom, is that "all power is given unto Me in heaven and earth." You know that it is not only Jesus Christ who is this all-powerful Being, but it is yourself as handiwork of an impartial God. Everything rises up near you to testify to your spreading righteousness. The golden text of this lesson, Acts 15: 12-29 tells the story of mental liberty from foreign notions as the free republic tells of freedom from former yokes; *"Through the grace of the Lord Jesus Christ we shall be saved, even as they."* (Verse 11)

It is as great a principle to proclaim that we are free from former religious and hindering beliefs as to proclaim that we will not be taxed without representation or permit a black man to be chased in the Everglades. If we think we have the perfect doctrine and the denominations are wrong, we are imprisoned into a mental belief which is mental stealing. For we certainly are mentally withholding from others their right to our idea that as sons of the same Father with us they know what is right as well as we do. We will hand them back the idea we have tried to steal away from them. We will give them our free knowledge that they are wise with the free wisdom of God.

We will probe the thought wells of our minds to still deeper teachings. If I thank God that He has given me my perfect hearing while I believe that He has made you to be deaf, I am taking away something from you with my mind. I am believing in a God who bestows and withholds. I am mentally stealing your rights. It is not praise of God I am giving when I look upon Him as any such being.

This mental giving up of former suppositions is taught by the ancient metaphysicians as the final freedom from stealing. It is a wonderful treatment to send over the ethers into the hearts of this age. The dark cloud that hangs over the planet through the mental unrest of mankind's feeling its bondage to something it knows not what, is the cloud that Washington saw. The teachings of Spiritual science will go to each heart and take out the wish to slay and torture from even the roughest and angriest, as the wise James poured oil on the Jews of this lesson. Peace will steal into their violent feelings by the free kindness of our beautiful teachings of the rights of all men to their transcendant wisdom and goodness. We do not need to speak aloud to the world concerning their rights any more than the good mental healer needs to speak aloud to the prisoner of paralysis. Thoughts go stealing like ointment into the clogged hopes of the world and mind is set free by the angels of light.

Now more than ever each event and each man tells you of your own freedom and the triumph of your own cause. Believe nothing that you may be free to believe all things. Think nothing, that you may think as the omniscient Mind of God.

With the abstaining from those things we have felt were our virtues, whereby we took from the free-handed Truth our realty by being grateful for blessing withholden from others, we are obeying the injunction of James in the twenty-ninth verse, *"Abstain from things strangled."* We have to be true to our principle of liberty for all men, even in the depth of our hearts. "For the Lord looketh on the heart." We do not think it is a virtue to give thanks to God for our home, our friends, our table, while we secretly steal from that same God the honor of believing that He has provided all creation with exactly the same blessings we have.

We let go our secret hold on the rights of the nations and silently shed abroad the final treatment of a closing age. If we let go our strangling ideas all the multitudes will lift up their heads with freedom, and long before Christmas, Christ, the Providing Jehovah, will be here, and there shall be no more pain or poverty, for the former earth is passed away.

December 11, 1892

LESSON XIII

Review of The Twelve Lessons

Claudius the fourth Emperor of Rome, was in the habit of exclaiming, "What! Do you take me for a fool?" The consequences was he lost his memory and became so absentminded that he did indeed appear like a fool to everyone. Suetonius, the historian of the Caesars, tells us that he inquired why Messalina, the Empress, did not come to the table, though she had been buried some days. He often ordered those whom he had condemned to death to dine with him the day after the execution, actually forgetting what had become of them and sending to reprimand them for their sluggishness in attending his banquets.

Thoughts often given expression to come due like notes or, like the planets in their orbits, reach perihelion (closest point to the Sun) on time. *"By thy words thou art justified"* (Matthew 12:37). Often we have people telling us that they nearly broke their neck trying to do certain things. They go away forgetting that such words are fishes' spawn and, though forgotten as the fishes forget their spawn, will some day throw them out of a carriage or down an embankment in a railway accident because their fruitage time has arrived.

Because you have forgotten your once familiar exclamations, do not be so silly as to suppose they will not arrive in your affairs at the proper moment. Violent expletives are making due haste to make violent conditions. All your adversaries are the legitimate offspring of such expressions as, "I thought I should die;" "I was nearly killed;" "I am utterly distracted."

Life words come up for reviews like soldiers well drilled. The lessons of the past quarter (of study) now file past our mental vision. If they were understood, they have already fruited, and new human environments now delight our once distraught hearts. For it is a point in pure Spiritual Science that every time a metaphysical proposition is clear to us we have a happy change of circumstances.

In our second lesson, we learned from the conversion of Saul by supernatural means that the scholastic world will either succumb to the Spiritual lightnings now striking them with palsy, softened brain, brittle bones, and will meekly recognize that it is spiritual lore they need instead of so much Sanskrit and pneumatics, or they will drop like shadows into nowhere.

It brought up the doctrine of Seneca, born in the year 7 B.C., that mankind must first get free from the bondage of death and then of poverty. It showed that if we set any limit to the action of the doctrine of Jesus we shall have some sort of ailment. For instance, if I do not believe that in the teaching that, *"My yoke is easy and my burden is light"* (Matthew 11:30), I am to be set into delightful pathways where all care, all anxiety, all effort is to be taken from me, I shall have something equivalent to Saul's blindness to mark my limitation of Jesus Christ's teachings.

No one was ever known to put any limitation upon the absolute demonstration of all the extreme statements of Jesus Christ who did not get hurt like Saul, who tried to limit the Christians, or did not finish up like Uzzah, who tried to stay with the ark. There is no miracle of interposition in your behalf out of the reach of your open acceptance of the extremest ideas of the transcendent doctrine of Jesus.

In the third lesson, the idea that we should never rehearse how well we used to do, nor tell how much we have turned off as skillful laborers in the past, was brought forward under the figure of Dorcas. It seems that talk of the past as superior to the present is sure death to our ambition and courage. The past exploits are not superior to this day's abilities. Rise like the transfiguring Spirit you are in your native splendor and tell of your powers and greatness this day. This is your Peter with his vigorous NOWNESS.

To be looking forward to great tasks that lie ahead of us is to be wearied in advance, like the pendulum in the fable, paralyzed like Aeneas, whom Peter cured by the idea of doing what belongs to us this moment, forgetting the past, ignoring the future. Evidently, Peter had covenanted with the Spirit to take care of his reputation and he would do nothing for it. He had covenanted with the Spirit to do every good work this moment. It is delightful to the Spirit to have us make a solid agreement to let it do all things now. This keeps a continual renewal of strength, vigor, health, life.

The fourth lesson taught that every sort of omen and prognostication is a prophecy of good. The world has always considered omens and signals to forbode death and disaster, but there was never one, which did not come expressly to foretell a great good. The way to meet an omen is to proclaim that it is a signal of new prosperities and renewed life. If evil came to a family after a strange phenomenon appeared, it was because the family twisted the promise from its beautiful purport.

Our fifth lesson teaches that we must take some line of high reasoning and stick to it. The descent from lofty descriptions of immaculate doctrines into small discussions of the foibles of people is accountable for many misfortunes and what are called ups and downs of life. Keep a certain set of statements for each hour in the day. The mind and character will soon translate from adversities into a constant succession of happy awakenings.

By our sixth lesson we were told that the usual missionary idea is totally wrong in that we go out to rescue men from the darkness of their ignorance, and the bondage of their sins. Going forth to seek lost souls is a subtle accusation against the creations of God. It is taught that as all is mind, of course, if we seek for ignorance we shall find it, but that law of seeking and finding does not make ignorance or sin reality. They will still remain imaginations of mind, not thinking as God thinks. Do you suppose God ever saw a heathen? No. He gave his own wisdom impartially to all mankind. Do you suppose God ever saw a sinner? No. He is too pure to behold iniquity. Then it is hunting *ignis fatuus* (with foolish passion) to be hunting out heathen and sinners. If we really love the South Sea Islanders we will praise them, not accuse them.

The next lesson taught how often it is the idea that we are not quite ready for carrying out projects which puts off other events from transpiring. Whatever the externals may seem, the mind should insist upon NOW for its own readiness to do all things. Then the externals will train to promptness.

It explains that we have our healing powers with their infinite endurance; our defending powers, with everlasting strength; but, like Peter's angel of defense, they depart after one miracle, leaving us in seeming powerlessness for a long time, because we keep wishing and longing for more, more, like Oliver Twist, instead of giving cheerful thanks continually for what we do have now, like as the wonderful Kurozumi practiced so successfully.

The eighth lesson asked us to consider whether we would have all the people of the world fed, clothed, sheltered, as the result of spiritual teachings with their miracle-working efficiencies, or slay and labor and fight for our chances on the present material basis. By spiritual means all these things are possible. Shall we throw our confidence upon the high seas of the Jesus Christ promises or hang back on the muddy bottoms of anguish with the striking world? Take the high winds of universal expectation. Narrow not your hopes down to your own lot alone. If the woman left alone in widowhood and poverty cast herself upon God to take care of her, and those who had to work for their living sent of their treasures to support her, do you not see that they in their turn would receive easy assistance by the same principle, and still others would receive their bounties the same way, till only the hosts of heaven should be found ministering to a whole world? Was not Jesus fed and clothed by the angels? If the angels can feed one man without killing some helpless animal, and clothe one man without a single man's forced labor, can they not feed and clothe a world? Are the hosts of God few? Are the hosts of God unwilling?

Our ninth lesson tells us not to get tied to our opinions, but to go from mountain top to mountain top of Truth till the freedom of the untrammeled God is ours. It asks us to consider whether this idea is a reasonable description of the experience of the Omnipotent, viz., "God suffers for sinners even more than they suffer themselves." No. Omnipotence is the Principle of absolute goodness, which neither itself suffers nor permits suffering. All suffering is delusion. That lesson taught plainly that Paul did not need to agree with prophecies of evil, thinking they must be fulfilled. He might trace their origin to an error and erase their whole history, as a metaphysician would erase the whole history of sickness from its first blunder to its externalization.

He must have a powerful mind arise with enough of the absolute Truth in his heart's faith to be perfectly well in his own body, renewed in youth by his doctrine, supported absolutely by his thoughts, so that the world may suddenly feel the almightiness of his doctrine by seeing his demonstrations. There shall not be one single breath in his speech or his writings about the power of a horde of opponents to darken his teachings; he shall not believe in any subtle region of his mind that he needs to protect himself from unjust or unkind thoughts; he shall not fear that he would come to want if he should give up his business or his goods; he shall not believe that an evil intention can possibly be carried out.

As Jesus came externalizing the hopes of ages, so the perfect doctrine shall bring forward its first perfect demonstration.

The tenth lesson explained that whoever will give the Spirit unresisted freedom through him will find himself expressing twelve powers, corresponding to the twelve gates of the heavenly city opened by right doctrine. Gentiles, or those without a particle of religious feeling of tradition, are as likely to express the twelve Jesus Christ powers, as Jews, or those who represent religious feeling and creed. It showed that every young man and young woman expects miracles to be wrought in his or her behalf, and if they would hold onto that expectation forever they would be forever young. They would be forever beautiful. It is not until they are tempted to be like the world by being pampered like Solomon or abused by experience with the way-wised of earth that they give utterly in to not expecting time to fulfill their confidence. They get the first wrinkles with agreeing with the deceptions, which read like the beginning of Johnson's "Rasselas."

The next lesson explained by the history of Kurozumi that there is an *elixir vitae* which we can breathe by learning how to do so. We set out with thoughts which reason out a noble doctrine. We let nothing interfere with our confidence in the Truth of our principles. Soon we get beyond thoughts. We enter the realm of the unnamed Good. We breathe the electric elixirs of a realm undescribed. We find our unmixed principles have power over our life quite beyond our first announcement. Mary, the mother of Jesus, brought Him forth by this high experience. Kuroaumi brought forth healing skill by it. We shall bring the heavenly Jerusalem of the Apocalypse into sight by our great number of men and women, with their eyes set on things of God, expecting the God beyond Him we have described to work for us.

Our twelfth lesson shows how Washington's sincerity brought an angel to tell him of things to come. He was permitted to see the liberation of America from foreign yoke. He was permitted to see the liberation of the colored South from the yoke of belief in slavery. He was permitted to see the hosts of heaven come in these days to liberate us from the belief in our limitations as human beings.

We are now being taught that we are transcendent beings with transcendent powers. We have no need to be limited by ignorance, poverty, sickness. We must take off the yoke of our supposition that there is any difference between the Hottentot and the college president in Spirit and in Truth.

We rise to proclaim that all men are the direct handiwork of impartial, glorious God. Every idea of this kind takes form and speeds on and on. Washington saw the field of Armageddon. We are now on that field. We do not believe in fighting; we believe as a people of God in letting the angels lift off the yokes. We do not believe in evil; we believe as a people in the angels of goodness, working our cause easily, swiftly, silently, by our unresisted confidence. If we experience hardships, it is because we have not taken refuge under the wings of our own doctrine.

December 18, 1892

CHRISTMAS LESSON

SHEPHERDS AND THE STAR

Luke 2:8-20

Part of lesson presumed given Christmas Day December 25, 1892

Why did the shepherds catch the gleams of a light that was not sunlight or moonlight or fire light? Because they were setting themselves free from the world-wide idea that some kind of material light must shine or they would be in darkness. Why did they have the songs of harmonious choirs whose soul-strung voices never had chanted of death or of mourning, but only of life and delight? Because for just a brief space they let alone the teachings of their schools and their churches concerning dying before seeing heavenly beings, and being resurrected before hearing of happiness as everywhere.

> *"Shepherds were watching their flocks by night, When far o'er the hills shown a beautiful light."*

That which was being enacted on the Jordan hills 1900 years ago is again taking place. Those who put to one side the "passes" of the doctrines of mankind are shepherds taking good care of their thoughts. The light that shines is the science of God now being taught. It has no trace of the sunlight or moonlight of former doctrine in its mysterious shining. To those who follow where it leads there is a young realization born. This realization of the divine power and divine harmony, waiting within each soul to be the arbiter of each life, is the young Jesus Christ.

No one has yet come into the manger with offerings of all his gold and frankincense and myrrh of property, genius, reputation. They who have the light shine round are those who think they will follow up the science and see where it leads. It will lead down to the meekness and lowliness of yielding up of will, love of praise, fear of blame, eagerness to be successful, into the mysterious manger of nothingness of such traditions.

He who does this is afterward lost as a shepherd of sheep. He is the Christ. He can work miracles. He shall not be a man with the idea of limited abilities. He shall be Jesus Christ with all power. He shall not reckon his age by years, his possessions by count, his health by state of flesh. He shall realize that before the world was he was, and without end is his ownership. His health and beauty are not reckoned by conditions of flesh, but by his mastership of flesh as Spirit.

There are a great number near the manger. They are now learning to give up their eagerness for praise, their fear of blame, their struggles to be ahead of their neighbors or to be of equal importance with the rest of the sound of the voice of Spirit. The "passes" of the world's competitions do not move them. They know that success must first be of the Spirit before it has any taste.

"Seek first the kingdom of God, and all these things shall be added."
"For we know that prosperity is of Thee."

It is now time for the light of Spiritual science to shine over the shepherds of the planet as it once shone over the shepherds of Judea.

As Mary was not Jesus Christ but only brought Him forth, so those who brought out this doctrine from the archives of the ages where it had been hidden are not Jesus Christ because they have not shown the miracle working power of Jesus Christ, the Spiritual science of his hour.

But as Mary yielded all things to Jesus, so those who preach it are now giving it its absolute freedom with their life. They are standing back and letting it demonstrate for itself. The knowledge which they bear in their bosom that it is omnipotent truth, is as much activity as they care to exhibit.

"Mary kept all these sayings and pondered them in her heart." We will each do our protecting duty by the young science, which never had any beginning but was with man from his first breath.

We will tell how true it is. We will tell its doctrines. We will praise its power. We will yield all we have, and are, to it till we are it absolutely. We shall prove that we are it only by our power of demonstrating in plain light of all mankind that there is no sin, no sickness, no death, no poverty, no feebleness, no senility, no mourning, for God is omnipresent and afflicted by none of these things.

December 25, 1892

Notes

Other Books by Emma Curtis Hopkins

- *Class Lessons of 1888 (WiseWoman Press)*
- *Bible Interpretations (WiseWoman Press)*
- *Esoteric Philosophy in Spiritual Science (WiseWoman Press)*
- *Genesis Series*
- *High Mysticism (WiseWoman Press)*
- *Self Treatments with Radiant I Am (WiseWoman Press)*
- *Gospel Series (WiseWoman Press)*
- *Judgment Series in Spiritual Science (WiseWoman Press)*
- *Drops of Gold (WiseWoman Press)*
- *Resume (WiseWoman Press)*
- *Scientific Christian Mental Practice (DeVorss)*

Books about Emma Curtis Hopkins and her teachings

- *Emma Curtis Hopkins, Forgotten Founder of New Thought* – Gail Harley
- *Unveiling Your Hidden Power: Emma Curtis Hopkins' Metaphysics for the 21st Century (also as a Workbook and as A Guide for Teachers)* – Ruth L. Miller
- *Power to Heal: Easy reading biography for all ages* –Ruth Miller

To find more of Emma's work, including some previously unpublished material, log on to:

www.emmacurtishopkins.com

WiseWoman Press

1521 NE Jantzen Ave #143
Portland, Oregon 97217
800.603.3005
www.wisewomanpress.com

Books Published by WiseWoman Press

By Emma Curtis Hopkins

- *Resume*
- *Gospel Series*
- *Class Lessons of 1888*
- *Self Treatments including Radiant I Am*
- *High Mysticism*
- *Esoteric Philosophy in Spiritual Science*
- *Drops of Gold Journal*
- *Judgment Series*
- *Bible Interpretations: Series I, II, III, IV, V, and VI*

By Ruth L. Miller

- *Unveiling Your Hidden Power: Emma Curtis Hopkins' Metaphysics for the 21st Century*
- *Coming into Freedom: Emily Cady's Lessons in Truth for the 21st Century*
- **150 Years of Healing: The Founders and Science of New Thought**
- *Power Beyond Magic: Ernest Holmes Biography*
- *Power to Heal: Emma Curtis Hopkins Biography*
- *The Power of Unity: Charles Fillmore Biography*
- *Uncommon Prayer*
- *Spiritual Success*
- *Finding the Path*

Watch our website for release dates and order information! - www.wisewomanpress.com

List of Bible Interpretation Series

with date from 1st to 14th Series.

This list is complete through the fourteenth Series. Emma produced at least thirty Series of Bible Interpretations.

She followed the Bible Passages provided by the International Committee of Clerics who produced the Bible Quotations for each year's use in churches all over the world.

Emma used these for her column of Bible Interpretations in both the Christian Science Magazine, at her Seminary and in the Chicago Inter-Ocean Newspaper.

First Series

July 5 - September 27, 1891

Lesson 1	The Word Made Flesh *John 1:1-18*	July 5th
Lesson 2	Christ's First Disciples John 1:29-42	July 12th
Lesson 3	All Is Divine Order *John 2:1-11* (Christ's first Miracle)	July 19th
Lesson 4	Jesus Christ and Nicodemus *John 3:1-17*	July 26th
Lesson 5	Christ at Samaria *John 4:5-26* (Christ at Jacob's Well)	August 2nd
Lesson 6	Self-condemnation *John 5:17-30* (Christ's Authority)	August 9th
Lesson 7	Feeding the Starving *John 6:1-14* (The Five Thousand Fed)	August 16th
Lesson 8	The Bread of Life *John 6:26-40* (Christ the Bread of Life)	August 23rd
Lesson 9	The Chief Thought *John 7:31-34* (Christ at the Feast)	August 30th
Lesson 10	Continue the Work *John 8:31-47*	September 6th
Lesson 11	Inheritance of Sin *John 9:1-11, 35-38* (Christ and the Blind Man)	September 13th
Lesson 12	The Real Kingdom *John 10:1-16* (Christ the Good Shepherd)	September 20th
Lesson 13	In Retrospection	September 27th Review

Second Series

October 4 - December 27, 1891

Lesson 1	Mary and Martha *John 11:21-44*	October 4th
Lesson 2	Glory of Christ *John 12:20-36*	October 11th
Lesson 3	Good in Sacrifice *John 13:1-17*	October 18th
Lesson 4	Power of the Mind *John 14:13; 15-27*	October 25th
Lesson 5	Vines and Branches *John 15:1-16*	November 1st
Lesson 6	Your Idea of God *John 16:1-15*	November 8th
Lesson 7	Magic of His Name *John 17:1-19*	November 15th
Lesson 8	Jesus and Judas *John 18:1-13*	November 22nd
Lesson 9	Scourge of Tongues *John 19:1-16*	November 29th
Lesson 10	Simplicity of Faith *John 19:17-30*	December 6th
Lesson 11	Christ is All in All *John 20: 1-18*	December 13th
Lesson 12	Risen With Christ *John 21:1-14*	December 20th
Lesson 13	The Spirit is Able Review of Year	December 27th

Third Series

January 3 - March 27, 1892

Lesson 1	A Golden Promise *Isaiah 11:1-10*	January 3rd
Lesson 2	The Twelve Gates *Isaiah 26:1-10*	January 10th
Lesson 3	Who Are Drunkards *Isaiah 28:1-13*	January 17th
Lesson 4	Awake Thou That Sleepest *Isaiah 37:1-21*	January 24th
Lesson 5	The Healing Light *Isaiah 53:1-21*	January 31st
Lesson 6	True Ideal of God *Isaiah 55:1-13*	February 7th
Lesson 7	Heaven Around Us *Jeremiah 31 14-37*	February 14th
Lesson 8	But One Substance *Jeremiah 36:19-31*	February 21st
Lesson 9	Justice of Jehovah *Jeremiah 37:11-21*	February 28th
Lesson 10	God and Man Are One *Jeremiah 39:1-10*	March 6th
Lesson 11	Spiritual Ideas *Ezekiel 4:9, 36:25-38*	March 13th
Lesson 12	All Flesh is Grass *Isaiah 40:1-10*	March 20th
Lesson 13	The Old and New Contrasted Review	March 27th

Fourth Series

April 3 - June 26, 1892

Lesson 1	Realm of Thought *Psalm 1:1-6*	April 3rd
Lesson 2	The Power of Faith *Psalm 2:1- 12*	April 10th
Lesson 3	Let the Spirit Work *Psalm 19:1-14*	April 17th
Lesson 4	Christ is Dominion *Psalm 23:1-6*	April 24th
Lesson 5	External or Mystic *Psalm 51:1-13*	May 1st
Lesson 6	Value of Early Beliefs *Psalm 72: 1-9*	May 8th
Lesson 7	Truth Makes Free *Psalm 84:1- 12*	May 15th
Lesson 8	False Ideas of God *Psalm 103:1-22*	May 22nd
Lesson 9	But Men Must Work *Daniel 1:8-21*	May 29th
Lesson 10	Artificial Helps *Daniel 2:36-49*	June 5th
Lesson 11	Dwelling in Perfect Life *Daniel 3:13-25*	June 12th
Lesson 12	Which Streak Shall Rule *Daniel 6:16-28*	June 19th
Lesson 13	See Things as They Are Review of 12 Lessons	June 26th

Fifth Series

July 3 - September 18, 1892

Lesson 1	The Measure of a Master *Acts 1:1-12*	July 3rd
Lesson 2	Chief Ideas Rule People *Acts 2:1-12*	July 10th
Lesson 3	New Ideas About Healing *Acts 2:37-47*	July 17th
Lesson 4	Heaven a State of Mind *Acts 3:1-16*	July 24th
Lesson 5	About Mesmeric Powers *Acts 4:1-18*	July 31st
Lesson 6	Points in the Mosaic Law *Acts 4:19-31*	August 7th
Lesson 7	Napoleon's Ambition *Acts 5:1-11*	August 14th
Lesson 8	A River Within the Heart *Acts 5:25-41*	August 21st
Lesson 9	The Answering of Prayer Acts 7: 54-60 - Acts 8: 1-4	August 28th
Lesson 10	Words Spoken by the Mind *Acts 8:5-35*	September 4th
Lesson 11	Just What It Teaches Us *Acts 8:26-40*	September 11th
Lesson 12	The Healing Principle Review	September 18th

Sixth Series

September 25 - December 18, 1892

Lesson 1	The Science of Christ *1 Corinthians 11:23-34*	September 25th
Lesson 2	On the Healing of Saul *Acts 9:1-31*	October 2nd
Lesson 3	The Power of the Mind Explained *Acts 9:32-43*	October 9th
Lesson 4	Faith in Good to Come *Acts 10:1-20*	October 16th
Lesson 5	Emerson's Great Task *Acts 10:30-48*	October 23rd
Lesson 6	The Teaching of Freedom *Acts 11:19-30*	October 30th
Lesson 7	Seek and Ye Shall Find *Acts 12:1-17*	November 6th
Lesson 8	The Ministry of the Holy Mother *Acts 13:1-13*	November 13th
Lesson 9	The Power of Lofty Ideas *Acts 13:26-43*	November 20th
Lesson 10	Sure Recipe for Old Age *Acts 13:44-52, 14:1-7*	November 27th
Lesson 11	The Healing Principle *Acts 14:8-22*	December 4th
Lesson 12	Washington's Vision *Acts 15:12-29*	December 11th
Lesson 13	Review of the Quarter	December 18th
Partial Lesson	Shepherds and the Star	December 25th

Seventh Series

January 1 - March 31, 1893

Lesson 1	All is as Allah Wills	January 1st
	Ezra 1	
	Khaled Knew that he was of The Genii	
	The Coming of Jesus	
Lesson 2	Zerubbabel's High Ideal	January 8th
	Ezra 2:8-13	
	Fulfillments of Prophecies	
	Followers of the Light	
	Doctrine of Spinoza	
Lesson 3	Divine Rays Of Power	January 15th
	Ezra 4	
	The Twelve Lessons of Science	
Lesson 4	Visions Of Zechariah	January 22nd
	Zechariah 3	
	Subconscious Belief in Evil	
	Jewish Ideas of Deity	
	Fruits of Mistakes	
Lesson 5	Aristotle's Metaphysician	January 27th
	Missing (See Review for summary)	
Lesson 6	The Building of the Temple	February 3rd
	Missing (See Review for summary)	
Lesson 7	Pericles and his Work in building the Temple	
	Nehemiah 13	February 12th
	Supreme Goodness	
	On and Upward	
Lesson 8	Ancient Religions	February 19th
	Nehemiah 1	
	The Chinese	
	The Holy Spirit	
Lesson 9	Understanding is Strength Part 1	February 26th
	Nehemiah 13	
Lesson 10	Understanding is Strength Part 2	March 3rd
	Nehemiah 13	
Lesson 11	Way of the Spirit	March 10th
	Esther	
Lesson 12	Speaking of Right Things	March 17th
		Proverbs 23:15-23
Lesson 13	Review	March 24th

Eighth Series

April 2 - June 25, 1893

Lesson 1	The Resurrection *Matthew 28:1-10* One Indestructible Life In Eternal Abundance The Resurrection Shakes Nature Herself Gospel to the Poor	April 2nd
Lesson 2	Universal Energy *Book of Job, Part 1*	April 9th
Lesson 3	Strength From Confidence *Book of Job, Part II*	April 16th
Lesson 4	The New Doctrine Brought Out *Book of Job, Part III*	April 23rd
Lesson 5	The Golden Text *Proverbs 1:20-23* Personification Of Wisdom Wisdom Never Hurts The "Two" Theory All is Spirit	April 30th
Lesson 6	The Law of Understanding *Proverbs 3* Shadows of Ideas The Sixth Proposition What Wisdom Promises Clutch On Material Things The Tree of Life Prolonging Illuminated Moments	May 7th
Lesson 7	Self-Esteem *Proverbs 12:1-15* Solomon on Self-Esteem The Magnetism of Passing Events Nothing Established by Wickedness Strength of a Vitalized Mind Concerning the "Perverse Heart"	May 14th

Lesson 8	Physical vs. Spiritual Power	May 21st
	Proverbs 23:29-35	
	Law of Life to Elevate the Good and Banish the Bad	
	Lesson Against Intemperance	
	Good Must Increase	
	To Know Goodness Is Life	
	The Angel of God's Presence	
Lesson 9	Lesson missing	May 28th
	(See Review for concept)	
Lesson 10	Recognizing Our Spiritual Nature	June 4th
	Proverbs 31:10-31	
	Was Called Emanuel	
	The covenant of Peace	
	The Ways of the Divine	
	Union With the Divine	
	Miracles Will Be Wrought	
Lesson 11	Intuition	June 11th
	Ezekiel 8:2-3	
	Ezekiel 9:3-6, 11	
	Interpretation of the Prophet	
	Ezekiel's Vision	
	Dreams and Their Cause	
	Israel and Judah	
	Intuition the Head	
	Our Limited Perspective	
Lesson 12	The Book of Malachi	June 18th
	Malachi	
	The Power of Faith	
	The Exercise of thankfulness	
	Her Faith Self-Sufficient	
	Burned with the Fires of Truth	
	What is Reality	
	One Open Road	
Lesson 13	Review of the Quarter	June 25th
	Proverbs 31:10-31	

Ninth Series

July 2 - September 27, 1893

Lesson 1	Secret of all Power	July 2nd
Acts 16: 6-15	The Ancient Chinese Doctrine of Taoism	
	Manifesting of God Powers	
	Paul, Timothy, and Silas	
	Is Fulfilling as Prophecy	
	The Inner Prompting.	
	Good Taoist Never Depressed	
Lesson 2	The Flame of Spiritual Verity	July 9th
Acts 16:18	Cause of Contention	
	Delusive Doctrines	
	Paul's History	
	Keynotes	
	Doctrine Not New	
Lesson 3	Healing Energy Gifts	July 16th
Acts 18:19-21	How Paul Healed	
	To Work Miracles	
	Paul Worked in Fear	
	Shakespeare's Idea of Loss	
	Endurance the Sign of Power	
Lesson 4	Be Still My Soul	July 23rd
Acts 17:16-24	Seeing Is Believing	
	Paul Stood Alone	
	Lessons for the Athenians	
	All Under His Power	
	Freedom of Spirit	
Lesson 5	(Missing) Acts 18:1-11	July 30th
Lesson 6	Missing No Lesson *	August 6th
Lesson 7	The Comforter is the Holy Ghost	August 13th
Acts 20	Requisite for an Orator	
	What is a Myth	
	Two Important Points	
	Truth of the Gospel	
	Kingdom of the Spirit	
	Do Not Believe in Weakness	

Lesson 8	Conscious of a Lofty Purpose	August 20th
Acts 21	As a Son of God	
	Wherein Paul failed	
	Must Give Up the Idea	
	Associated with Publicans	
	Rights of the Spirit	
Lesson 9	Measure of Understanding	August 27th
Acts 24:19-32	Lesser of Two Evils	
	A Conciliating Spirit	
	A Dream of Uplifting	
	The Highest Endeavor	
	Paul at Caesarea	
	Preparatory Symbols	
	Evidence of Christianity	
Lesson 10	The Angels of Paul	September 3rd
Acts 23:25-26	Paul's Source of Inspiration	
	Should Not Be Miserable	
	Better to Prevent than Cure	
	Mysteries of Providence	
Lesson 11	The Hope of Israel	September 10th
Acts 28:20-31	Immunity for Disciples	
	Hiding Inferiorities	
	Pure Principle	
Lesson 12	Joy in the Holy Ghost	September 17th
Romans 14	Temperance	
	The Ideal Doctrine	
	Tells a Different Story	
	Hospitals as Evidence	
	Should Trust in the Savior	
Lesson 13	Review	September 24th
Acts 26-19-32	The Leveling Doctrine	
	Boldness of Command	
	Secret of Inheritance	
	Power in a Name	

Tenth Series

October 1 – December 24, 1893

Lesson 1	*Romans 1:1-19*	October 1st
	When the Truth is Known	
	Faith in God	
	The Faithful Man is Strong	
	Glory of the Pure Motive	
Lesson 2	*Romans 3:19-26*	October 8th
	Free Grace.	
	On the Gloomy Side	
	Daniel and Elisha	
	Power from Obedience	
	Fidelity to His Name	
	He Is God	
Lesson 3	*Romans 5*	October 15th
	The Healing Principle	
	Knows No Defeat.	
	In Glorified Realms	
	He Will Come	
Lesson 4	*Romans 12:1*	October 22nd
	Would Become Free	
	Man's Co-operation	
	Be Not Overcome	
	Sacrifice No Burden	
	Knows the Future	
Lesson 5	*I Corinthians 8:1-13*	October 29th
	The Estate of Man	
	Nothing In Self	
	What Paul Believed	
	Doctrine of Kurozumi	
Lesson 6	*I Corinthians 12:1-26*	November 5th
	Science of The Christ Principle	
	Dead from the Beginning	
	St. Paul's Great Mission	
	What The Spark Becomes	
	Chris, All There Is of Man	
	Divinity Manifest in Man	
	Christ Principle Omnipotent	

Lesson 7	*II Corinthians 8:1-12*	November 12th
	Which Shall It Be?	
	The Spirit is Sufficient	
	Working of the Holy Ghost	
Lesson 8	*Ephesians 4:20-32*	November 19th
	A Source of Comfort	
	What Causes Difference of Vision	
	Nothing But Free Will	
Lesson 9	*Colossians 3:12-25*	November 26th
	Divine in the Beginning	
	Blessings of Contentment	
	Free and Untrammeled Energy	
Lesson 10	*James 1*	December 3rd
	The Highest Doctrine	
	A Mantle of Darkness	
	The Counsel of God	
	Blessed Beyond Speaking	
Lesson 11	*I Peter 1*	December 10th
	Message to the Elect	
	Not of the World's Good	
Lesson 12	*Revelation 1:9*	December 17th
	Self-Glorification	
	The All-Powerful Name	
	Message to the Seven Churches	
	The Voice of the Spirit	
Lesson 13	Golden Text	December 24th
	Responding Principle Lives	
	Principle Not Hidebound	
	They Were Not Free Minded	
Lesson 14	Review	December 31st
	It is Never Too Late	
	The Just Live by Faith	
	An Eternal Offer	
	Freedom of Christian Science	

Eleventh Series

January 1 – March 25, 1894

Lesson 1	*Genesis 1:26-31 & 2:1-3*	January 7th
	The First Adam	
	Man: The Image of Language Paul and Elymas	
Lesson 2	*Genesis 3:1-15*	January 14th
	Adam's Sin and God's Grace	
	The Fable of the Garden	
	Looked-for Sympathy	
	The True Doctrine	
Lesson 3	*Genesis 4:3-13*	January 21st
	Types of the Race	
	God in the Murderer	
	God Nature Unalterable	
Lesson 4	*Genesis 9:8-17*	January 28th
	God's Covenant With Noah	
	Value of Instantaneous Action	
	The Lesson of the Rainbow	
Lesson 5	I Corinthians 8:1-13	February 4th
	Genesis 12:1-9	
	Beginning of the Hebrew Nation	
	No Use For Other Themes	
	Influence of Noble Themes	
	Danger In Looking Back	
Lesson 6	*Genesis 17:1-9*	February 11th
	God's Covenant With Abram	
	As Little Children	
	God and Mammon	
	Being Honest With Self	
Lesson 7	*Genesis 18:22-23*	February 18th
	God's Judgment of Sodom	
	No Right Nor Wrong In Truth	
	Misery Shall Cease	
Lesson 8	*Genesis 22:1-13*	February 25th
	Trial of Abraham's Faith	
	Light Comes With Preaching	
	You Can Be Happy NOW	

Lesson 9	*Genesis 25:27-34*	March 4th
	Selling the Birthright	
	"Ye shall be Filled"	
	The Delusion Destroyed	
Lesson 10	*Genesis 28:10-22*	March 11th
	Jacob at Bethel	
	Many Who Act Like Jacob	
	How to Seek Inspiration	
	Christ, the True Pulpit Orator	
	The Priceless Knowledge of God	
Lesson 11	*Proverbs 20:1-7*	March 18th
	Temperance	
	Only One Lord	
	What King Alcohol Does	
	Stupefying Ideas	
Lesson 12	*Mark 16:1-8*	March 25th
	Review and Easter	
	Words of Spirit and Life	
	Facing the Supreme	
	Erasure of the Law	
	Need No Other Friend	

Twelfth Series

April 1 – June 24, 1894

Lesson 1	*Genesis 24:30, 32:09-12*	April 8th
	Jacob's Prevailing Prayer	
	God Transcends Idea	
	All To Become Spiritual	
	Ideas Opposed to Each Other	April 1st
Lesson 2	*Genesis 37:1-11*	
	Discord in Jacob's Family	
	Setting Aside Limitations	
	On the Side of Truth	
Lesson 3	*Genesis 37:23-36*	April 15th
	Joseph Sold into Egypt	
	Influence on the Mind	
	Of Spiritual Origin	
Lesson 4	*Genesis 41:38-48*	April 22nd
	Object Lesson Presented in	
	the Book of Genesis	
Lesson 5	*Genesis 45:1-15*	April 29th
	"With Thee is Fullness of Joy"	
	India Favors Philosophic Thought	
	What These Figures Impart	
	The Errors of Governments	
Lesson 6	*Genesis 50:14-26*	May 6th
	Changes of Heart	
	The Number Fourteen	
	Divine Magicians	
Lesson 7	*Exodus 1:1-14*	May 13th
	Principle of Opposites	
	Power of Sentiment	
	Opposition Must Enlarge	
Lesson 8	*Exodus 2:1-10*	May 20th
	How New Fires Are Enkindled	
	Truth Is Restless	
	Man Started from God	
Lesson 9	*Exodus 3:10-20*	May 27th
	What Science Proves	
	What Today's Lesson Teaches	
	The Safety of Moses	

Lesson 10	*Exodus 12:1-14*	June 3rd
	The Exodus a Valuable Force	
	What the Unblemished Lamp Typifies	
	Sacrifice Always Costly	
Lesson 11	*Exodus 14:19-29*	June 10th
	Aristides and Luther Contrasted	
	The Error of the Egyptians	
	The Christian Life not Easy	
	The True Light Explained	
Lesson 12	*Proverbs 23:29-35*	June 17th
	Heaven and Christ will Help	
	The Woes of the Drunkard	
	The Fight Still Continues	
	The Society of Friends	
Lesson 13	*Proverbs 23:29-35*	June 24th
	Review	
	Where is Man's Dominion	
	Wrestling of Jacob	
	When the Man is Seen	

Thirteenth Series

July 1 – September 30, 1894

Lesson 1	The Birth of Jesus	July 1st
	Luke 2:1-16	
	No Room for Jesus	
	Man's Mystic Center	
	They glorify their Performances	
Lesson 2	Presentation in the Temple	July 8th
	Luke 2:25-38	
	A Light for Every Man	
	All Things Are Revealed	
	The Coming Power	
	Like the Noonday Sun	
Lesson 3	Visit of the Wise Men	July 15th
	Matthew 1:2-12	
	The Law Our Teacher	
	Take neither Scrip nor Purse	
	The Star in the East	
	The Influence of Truth	
Lesson 4	Flight Into Egypt	July 22nd
	Mathew 2:13-23	
	The Magic Word of Wage Earning	
	How Knowledge Affect the Times	
	The Awakening of the Common People	
Lesson 5	The Youth of Jesus	July 29th
	Luke2:40-52	
	Your Righteousness is as filthy Rags	
	Whatsoever Ye Search, that will Ye Find	
	The starting Point of All Men	
	Equal Division, the Lesson Taught by Jesus	
	The True Heart Never Falters	
Lesson 6	The "All is God" Doctrine	August 5th
	Luke 2:40-52	
	Three Designated Stages of Spiritual Science	
	Christ Alone Gives Freedom	
	The Great Leaders of Strikes	
Lesson 7	Missing	August 12th
Lesson 8	First Disciples of Jesus	August 19th
	John 1:36-49	
	The Meaning of Repentance	

	Erase the Instructed Mind	
	The Necessity of Rest	
	The Self-Center No Haltered Joseph	
Lesson 9	The First Miracle of Jesus	August 26th
	John 2:1-11	
	"I Myself am Heaven or Hell"	
	The Satan Jesus Recognized	
	The Rest of the People of God	
	John the Beholder of Jesus	
	The Wind of the Spirit	
Lesson 10	Jesus Cleansing the Temple	September 2nd
	John 2:13-25	
	The Secret of Fearlessness	
	Jerusalem the Symbol of Indestructible Principle	
	What is Required of the Teacher	
	The Whip of Soft Cords	
Lesson 11	Jesus and Nicodemus	September 9th
	John 3:1-16	
	Metaphysical Teaching of Jesus	
	Birth-Given Right of Equality	
	Work of the Heavenly Teacher	
Lesson 12	Jesus at Jacob's Well	September 16th
	John 4:9-26	
	The Question of the Ages	
	The Great Teacher and Healer	
	"Because I Live, Ye shall Live Also."	
	The Faith That is Needful	
Lesson 13	Daniel's Abstinence	September 23rd
	Daniel 1:8-20	
	Knowledge is Not All	
	Between the Oriental and Occidental Minds	
	The Four Servants of God	
	The Saving Power of Good	
	The Meeting-Ground of Spirit and Truth	
Lesson 14	Take With You Words	September 30th
	John 2:13-25	
Review	Healing Comes from Within	
	The Marthas and Marys of Christianity	
	The Summing up of The Golden Texts	

Fourteenth Series

October 7 – December 30, 1894

Lesson 1	Jesus At Nazareth	October 7th
Luke 4:16-30	Jesus Teaches Uprightness	
	The Pompous Claim of a Teacher	
	The Supreme One No Respecter of Persons	
	The Great Awakening	
	The Glory of God Will Come Back	
Lesson 2	The Draught of Fishes	October 14th
Luke 5:1-11	The Protestant Within Every Man	
	The Cry of Those Who Suffer	
	Where the Living Christ is Found	
Lesson 3	The Sabbath in Capernaum	October 21st
Mark 1:21-34	Why Martyrdom Has Been a Possibility	
	The Truth Inculcated in Today's Lesson	
	The Injustice of Vicarious Suffering	
	The Promise of Good Held in the Future	
Lesson 4	The Paralytic Healed	October 28th
Mark 2:1-12	System Of Religions and Philosophy	
	The Principle Of Equalization	
	The Little Rift In School Methods	
	What Self-Knowledge Will Bring	
	The Meaning Of The Story of Capernaum	
Lesson 5	Reading of Sacred Books	November 4th
Mark 2:23-38	The Interior Qualities	
Mark 2:1-4	The Indwelling God	
	Weakness Of The Flesh	
	The Unfound Spring	
Lesson 6	Spiritual Executiveness	November 11th
Mark 3:6-19	The Teaching Of The Soul	
	The Executive Powers Of The Mind	
	Vanity Of Discrimination	
	Truth Cannot Be Bought Off	
	And Christ Was Still	
	The Same Effects For Right And Wrong	
	The Unrecognized Splendor Of The Soul	

Lesson 7	Twelve Powers Of The Soul	November 18th
Luke 6:20-31	The Divine Ego in Every One	
	Spiritual Better than Material Wealth	
	The Fallacy Of Rebuke	
	Andrew, The Unchanging One	
Lesson 8	Things Not Understood Attributed to Satan	
Mark 3:22-35	True Meaning Of Hatha Yoga	November 25th
	The Superhuman Power Within Man	
	The Problem of Living and Prospering	
	Suffering Not Ordained for Good	
	The Lamb in the Midst shall Lead	
Lesson 9	Independence of Mind	December 2nd
Luke 7:24-35	He that Knoweth Himself Is Enlightened	
	The Universal Passion for Saving Souls	
	Strength From knowledge of Self	
	Effect Of Mentally Directed Blows	
Lesson 10	The Gift of Untaught wisdom	December 9th
Luke 8:4-15	The Secret Of Good Comradeship	
	The Knower That Stands in Everyone	
	Laying Down the Symbols	
	Intellect The Devil Which Misleads	
	Interpretation Of The Day's Lesson	
Lesson 11	The Divine Eye Within	December 16th
Matthew 5:5-16	Knowledge Which Prevails Over Civilization	
	The Message Heard By Matthew	
	The Note Which shatters Walls Of Flesh	
Lesson 12	Unto Us a Child Is Born	December 23rd
Luke 7:24-35	The Light That is Within	
	Significance Of The Vision of Isaiah	
	Signs of the Times	
	The New Born Story Of God	
	Immaculate Vision Impossible To None	
Lesson 13	Review	December 30th
Isaiah 9:2-7	That Which Will Be Found In The Kingdom	
	Situation Of Time And Religion Reviewed	
	Plea That Judgment May Be Righteous	
	The Souls Of All One And Changeless	

www.ingramcontent.com/pod-product-compliance
Lightning Source LLC
Chambersburg PA
CBHW062226080426
42734CB00010B/2044